CliffsN

The Awakening

By Maureen Kelly

IN THIS BOOK

- Learn about the Life and Background of the Author

- Preview an Introduction to the Novel

- Explore themes, character development, and recurring images in the Critical Commentaries

- Examine in-depth Character Analyses

- Acquire an understanding of the work with Critical Essays

- Reinforce what you learn with CliffsNotes Review

- Find additional information to further your study in CliffsNotes Resource Center and online at www.cliffsnotes.com

Wiley Publishing, Inc.

About the Author
Maureen Kelly is a freelance writer and editor.

Publisher's Acknowledgments
Editorial
Project Editor: Tere Drenth
Acquisitions Editor: Greg Tubach
Glossary Editors: The editors and staff at Webster's New World™ Dictionaries
Editorial Administrator: Michelle Hacker
Production
Indexer: York Production Services, Inc.
Proofreader: York Production Services, Inc.
Wiley Indianapolis Composition Services

CliffsNotes™ *The Awakening*

Published by:
Wiley Publishing, Inc.
909 Third Avenue
New York, NY 10022
www.wiley.com

Copyright © 2001 Wiley Publishing, Inc., New York, New York
Library of Congress Control Number: 00-107790
ISBN: 0-7645-8652-1
Printed in the United States of America
10 9 8 7 6 5 4 3
1O/TQ/QY/QS/IN
Published by Wiley Publishing, Inc., New York, NY
Published simultaneously in Canada

Table of Contents

How to Use This Book

CliffsNotes *The Awakening* supplements the original work, giving you background information about the author, an introduction to the novel, a graphical character map, critical commentaries, expanded glossaries, and a comprehensive index. CliffsNotes Review tests your comprehension of the original text and reinforces learning with questions and answers, practice projects, and more. For further information on Kate Chopin and *The Awakening*, check out the CliffsNotes Resource Center.

CliffsNotes provides the following icons to highlight essential elements of particular interest:

Reveals the underlying themes in the work.

Helps you to more easily relate to or discover the depth of a character.

Uncovers elements such as setting, atmosphere, mystery, passion, violence, irony, symbolism, tragedy, foreshadowing, and satire.

Enables you to appreciate the nuances of words and phrases.

Don't Miss Our Web Site

Discover classic literature as well as modern-day treasures by visiting the CliffsNotes Web site at www.cliffsnotes.com. You can obtain a quick download of a CliffsNotes title, purchase a title in print form, browse our catalog, or view online samples.

You'll also find interactive tools that are fun and informative, links to interesting Web sites, tips, articles, and additional resources to help you, not only for literature, but for test prep, finance, careers, computers, and the Internet too. See you at www.cliffsnotes.com!

LIFE AND BACKGROUND OF THE AUTHOR

Personal Background

Kate Chopin was born Catherine O'Flaherty in St. Louis on February 8, 1850. Her mother, Eliza Faris, came from an old French family that lived outside of St. Louis. Her father, Thomas, was a highly successful Irish-born businessman; he died when Kate was five years old. Chopin grew up in a household dominated by women: her mother, great-grandmother, and the female slaves her mother owned, who took care of the children. Young Chopin spent a lot of time in the attic reading such masters as Jane Austen, Charles Dickens, and the Brontës. Her great-grandmother taught her to speak French and play piano, and related stories about her great-great-grandmother, a woman who ran her own business, was separated from her husband, and had children while unmarried. This woman great example for young Katie of a woman's strength, potential for independence, and the real workings of life's passions.

Like the rest of her family, Chopin grew up strongly pro-Confederate, a sentiment enhanced by her beloved half-brother's death in the Civil War. In fact, 13-year-old Chopin was arrested when she tore a Union flag from her family's porch that had been hung there by the triumphant Union troops. She became known as St. Louis's "Littlest Rebel"—a trait that marked Chopin's behavior as an adult, when she attended her own interests more closely than society's arbitrary and sexist dictates.

Education

Chopin attended a St. Louis Catholic girl's school, Academy of the Sacred Heart, from ages five to eighteen. There, the nuns continued the female-oriented education begun at home by her great-grandmother, providing a forum for their students to express their thoughts and share their opinions.

Marriage and Children

After finishing her education at Academy of the Sacred Heart, Chopin entered St. Louis society, where she met Oscar Chopin, a French-born *cotton factor* (the middleman between cotton grower and buyer). She married Oscar in June 1870, and they moved to New Orleans. Between 1871 and 1879, she had six children. Like Edna and Léonce Pontellier, the Chopins vacationed during summers on Grand

Isle, to avoid the cholera outbreaks in the city of New Orleans. Also like Edna, Chopin took long walks alone in New Orleans, often while smoking cigarettes, much to the astonishment of passersby.

When Oscar's cotton brokerage business failed due to drought and his mismanagement, they moved to the small French village of Cloutierville, Louisiana where Oscar had family and a small amount of land. Chopin was distinguished in this tiny town by her habit of riding horses astride rather than sidesaddle, dressing too fashionably for her surroundings, and smoking cigarettes—all of which were considered unladylike. Many of the locals found their way into her later stories.

Oscar ran a general store in Cloutierville until he died in 1882 of malaria. Upon his death, which left his family in great debt, Chopin ran the store and their small plantation, a highly unusual move for widows at the time. Not until 1884 did Chopin take the usual course for widows, when she and her children moved back to St. Louis to live with her mother. Before she left Cloutierville, Chopin had an affair with a local married man who is said to be the prototype for Alcée Arobin in *The Awakening*.

Her Later Years

A year after Chopin moved her family back to St. Louis, she began to write, publishing first a piece of music called "Polka for Piano" in 1888 and then a poem called "If It Might Be" in 1889. She then turned her attention toward fiction and concentrated on that genre for the rest of her life.

Resenting the expectation that she was to spend her days making social calls on other women, Chopin began St. Louis's first literary salon, a social gathering one evening a week where both women and men could gather for some intelligent conversation. Through these salons, she fulfilled the social requirement to entertain regularly but did so under her own terms. A benefit of these salons was professional advancement: Publishers and reviewers alike attended Chopin's salons, providing a fertile network for the ambitious Chopin to pursue additional publication opportunities.

Chopin published almost 100 short stories, three novels, and one play within twelve years—after she began writing, she pursued it with the same business sense she displayed while running her husband's general store after he died.

In her last years, health problems made writing difficult, although many people attributed the decrease in her writing as a result of the storm of negative publicity that accompanied *The Awakening*'s publication in 1899. Her death came suddenly; she died on August 22, 1904 of a massive cerebral hemorrhage.

Literary Writing

Chopin's first short story was published in 1889; she began her first novel, *At Fault*, that year as well. Chopin was assiduous about submitting manuscripts and cultivating relationships with influential editors. Her stories appeared in prestigious magazines such as *Vogue* and *Atlantic Monthly*, and two collections of her short stories were published in book form, as *Bayou Folk* (1894) and *A Night in Acadie* (1897). Both of those books were well received, although regarded by many reviewers and critics primarily as "regionalist" work, meaning it had little literary value beyond the portrait it presented of the Louisiana/Missouri region.

Her most famous work, *The Awakening*, appeared in 1899. As in much of Chopin's writing, this novel concerns itself with issues of identity and morality. Unlike the rest of her work, it created a tremendous controversy. While many reviewers deemed it a worthy novel, an equal and more vocal number condemned it, not simply for Edna's behavior, but for her lack of remorse about her behavior—and Chopin's refusal to judge Edna either way.

A well-regarded author at the time of her death, despite the controversy surrounding *The Awakening*, Chopin's work fell into obscurity for many years as regional literature fell out of literary favor. Chopin's work did not come to the attention of the established literary world until 1969, after almost 70 years of obscurity, with the publication of Per Seyersted's critical biography and his edition of her complete works. The 1960s feminist movement in America had a great deal to do with her new-found fame as well; that movement brought to attention the work of women who had been excluded from the literary canon by its male creators. Today, her work is part of the canon of American literature.

INTRODUCTION TO THE NOVEL

Introduction

The Awakening has enjoyed a strange success: At the time of its publication, critics condemned the novel for its heroine's unrepentant drive for independence and emotional, sexual, and spiritual awakening. Although contrary to legend it was never a banned book, the novel fell into obscurity for 70 years. Read in the radical context of the 1960s, *The Awakening* was received enthusiastically as a valid work; the scandal that destroyed its chance of success at the time of its publication seemed absurd.

A scandal usually secures a book's success, particularly when a book is accused not only of describing immorality but also of promoting it—typically in such a situation, everyone wants to find out what they're not supposed to hear or know. This phenomenon did not occur with *The Awakening*, however, possibly because Edna's story was just too depressing: She is not a character made two dimensional by excessive virtue or vice; rather, she achieves a certain realism in her character's mixture of flaws and features. She's too real, and readers found it too sad that she must kill herself to finally elude society's demand that she be a mother first and a human being second. Female readers in 1899 did not find an easy escape out of their own lives when they picked up *The Awakening*—entering Edna's life, they were forced to understand her choices and lack of them, and re-encounter the same limitations that marked their own lives.

Many male reviewers condemned *The Awakening* primarily out of fear of the very real shifting in the social order. Women were still required by society to live and uphold the mother-woman role, but at the same time, they were increasingly choosing to work outside the home. The suffrage movement was in full swing, threatening the masculine grip on the realms of politics and economics. While Edna is no suffragette, evidencing no interest in any cause other than her own intensely personal agenda, her rejection of the mother-woman role, exploration of her sexuality with men other than her husband, and indifference to the opinions of mainstream society make her threatening indeed to those readers who wished women would remain at home.

The suffragettes were not the only force making waves for the mainstream. Charlotte Perkins Gilman wrote the groundbreaking *Women and Economics*, published in 1898, which viewed marriage with an economic perspective: A wife pays for her room and board in her husband's house by bearing his children, rendering sexual reproduction an economic function and the American family nothing more than a system of barter. Edna attempts to exit this system by funding her own little household but still cannot escape its grip—hardly good news for those women who agreed with Gilman's analysis.

Edna's status as a *trophy wife*—a woman whose life of leisure is a testament to her husband's financial success—is essential to her development, however. Because she has servants to attend to necessary household tasks and take care of her children, she can devote time to art, solitary reflection, and the influential relationships. Reviewers from the 1970s until the present note that the servants in Edna's household are rarely heard to speak, and frequently their names are not given. The lack of attention in the novel to the servant women's perspectives tells a great deal in the omission—if Edna could not free herself from the role society cast her in, how much more difficult must it have been for those women trapped in Louisiana's elaborate racial caste system. Only a few short decades after the Civil War, Louisiana retained its intensely bigoted environment and practices.

In addition, the sexism associated with the antebellum South was alive and well for Chopin and Edna. In highly conservative Louisiana, women were expected to behave as stereotypical Southern belles, pure of heart and chaste in action. Such a role symbolically prohibited an active place in public life. Literal constraints were in place, as well, such as the law that declared married women, along with children and the mentally ill, incompetent to initiate or complete legal contracts. As an independent-minded woman and native of St. Louis, Chopin drew on her own experiences as an outsider in Louisiana to flesh out Edna's portrait as a scandalously independent woman. Like Edna, Chopin sought to create her own life, such as instituting a literary salon to replace all the other social visits society expected her to pay. However, unlike Edna, Chopin was very much at home in her independence.

Literary Limitations

Part of the scandal surrounding the novel was Chopin's bold choice of female self-discovery and self-reliance. Women writers, throughout the United States but particularly in the South, were expected to stick with ladylike subjects; a portrayal of female sexuality or intense dissatisfaction with their married lives was not on that list. Further, because Chopin used Louisiana so frequently in her stories, she was marginalized as a *regional writer,* a term used for writers who vividly describe the local color but don't necessarily produce great literature. When male writers, such as Mark Twain, drew heavily on their surroundings for character or theme, their work was understood to be literature that made use of certain regional characteristics to great effect, rather than simply a description of those characteristics, as is the case with regional writers. As a woman, Chopin's status as a writer was severely limited by the expectations of an intensely chauvinistic public. When she shattered all expectations by producing a work that clearly transcended not only regionalism but also the established list of sentimental subjects thought suitable for women, the furor was intense.

In Edna Pontellier's America, female sexuality was an utterly taboo subject. For women, sex was supposed to be a means to one specific end: making babies within the context of marriage. Part of the reason Edna's behavior seemed so scandalous at the time was that her sexuality neither began nor ended with her husband as the times dictated it ought; she discovered it with other men after she was already married.

Further, Edna advances not only in knowledge of her sexuality but also in awareness of her spirituality: Upon moving into the pigeon house, she has a sense "of having descended in the social scale, with a corresponding sense of having risen in the spiritual." This increase in her spiritual stock occurs *after* she has begun her affair with Arobin, a point at which a standard heroine of the times should have felt irredeemably shamed and certainly less spiritually advanced.

Edna's sexual awakening is doubtless a reflection of the sexuality glorified in Walt Whitman's landmark poetry of self-celebration, *Leaves of Grass*, the imagery or influence of which is frequently found in *The Awakening*. One of Whitman's most famous lines reads "If I worship one thing more than another it shall be the spread of my own body, or any part of it." That sentiment is manifest in Edna's new appreciation for her body that occurs during her day at Madame Antoine's. *Leaves of Grass* outraged the public's puritanical sensibilities in 1855 with its male author's celebration of sensuality; how much worse for a woman to celebrate her self and sexuality, even 44 years later.

Another troubling factor for Chopin's contemporaries was her refusal to condemn Edna. She describes Edna's actions and reactions without passing judgment, a literary device that precedes the modernist literature of the 1920s by two decades. After kissing Arobin for the first time, Edna felt "neither shame nor remorse" and Chopin doesn't suggest that she should. Instead, using a narrative voice distant and ambiguous in tone, she presents Edna's development and decisions without the moralizing that was expected from novelists. Book and magazine editors of the time routinely asked writers to maintain a certain moral tone in their work, or at least provide endings for their heroines that were in keeping with the accepted avenues: Women were to be married off or, if left solitary, remain virginal. Many reviewers described Chopin's novel with terms such as "unhealthy" and "morbid." One review declared that "*The Awakening* is too strong drink for moral babes, and should be labeled 'poison.'"

The Influence of Science

Part of Chopin's reluctance to pass judgment using the established moral codes may have stemmed from the scientific advancements of the last half of the 1800s. The work of Charles Darwin and his supporters fundamentally changed, or at least challenged, the way people thought about who they were, where they came from, and where they were going. The very idea of evolution necessitated a fundamental shift in thinking, casting previously ironclad ideas into doubt. So, too, does Chopin depict Edna's shift in perspective as causing an irreparable break with her former life, disallowing the possibility that she can simply move back into Léonce's house and resume her limiting life.

The Influence of Naturalism and Romanticism

Given Chopin's approach to the novel, there can be no happy ending for Edna, and this feature places *The Awakening* in the naturalist school of writing. Established in the last half of the nineteenth century, Naturalist and the closely associated Realist literature held that writing should offer an objective, empirical presentation of the human experience. Naturalism required an amoral stance towards a character's actions and aspirations—but nonetheless expected the worst both for and from the character. The influence of Darwin's theories on naturalism resulted in the sentiment that humans have little control over themselves or the forces that shape their lives, but must struggle to survive, prospering only at the expense of others. As if to emphasize that she is consciously including that school's principles or approach in her novel, Chopin has Edna reading a novel by the realist writer Edmund Goncourt.

In stark contrast with naturalism was the much older school of romanticism, which promoted the idea that anyone's life or worldview could be transformed by idealism and self-knowledge. American romanticism put an emphasis on the role of art in such a transformation. Ironically, *The Awakening* was heavily influenced by this school, as well:

Chopin presents a character whose relationship with art both engenders and indicates her life's transformation. Although Edna is not a serious artist, her art does reflect her growth as a person. Her focus on developing her spiritual rather than material state is in keeping with the related transcendentalist philosophy of Emerson and Thoreau; in fact, Edna is shown reading Emerson her first night alone in the mansion. Transcendentalist writers, themselves influenced by the romantics, have an optimistic view about human potential and express the need to appreciate independence in spirit and action, even when in conflict with mainstream expectations. As Edna learns her own mind and follows her heart, defying her culture's traditions and orthodoxy, she is exemplifying the values of transcendentalism.

By presenting a heroine who attempts to transform her life but ultimately feels overwhelmed by those around her and defeated by herself, Chopin depicts the dark side, what cynics would call the *realistic consequences,* of Edna's romantic impulse to reconfigure her life according to her own true principles.

Chopin's novel arrived at a pivotal juncture in time: The roots of feminism had been established in the 1890s but the future of women's economic, political, and personal independence was far from determined. Just so Edna's life, which indicates the real possibility of a new independence but does not promise that such independence will be easily won or maintained.

A Brief Synopsis

The Awakening explores one woman's desire to find and live fully within her true self. Her devotion to that purpose causes friction with her friends and family, and also conflicts with the dominant values of her time.

Edna Pontellier's story takes place in 1890s Louisiana, within the upper-class Creole society. Edna, her husband Léonce, and their two children are vacationing for the summer on Grand Isle, an island just off the Louisiana shore near New Orleans. They are staying at a *pension*, a sort of boarding house where each family has their own cottage but eat together in a main dining hall. Also staying at the *pension* is the Ratignolle family; Madame Ratignolle is a close friend of Edna's, although their philosophies and attitudes toward child rearing differ fundamentally. Madame Ratignolle is the epitome of a "mother-woman," gladly sacrificing a distinct personal identity to devote her entire being to the care of her children, husband, and household.

In contrast to Madame Ratignolle's character is Mademoiselle Reisz, a brilliant pianist also vacationing on Grand Isle. Although Mademoiselle Reisz offends almost everyone with her brutal assessments of others, she likes Edna, and they become friends. Mademoiselle Reisz's piano performance stirs Edna deeply, awakening her capacity for passion and engendering the process of personal discovery that Edna undertakes—almost accidentally—that summer.

Another Grand Isle vacationer is the young and charming Robert Lebrun. Robert devotes himself each summer season to a different woman, usually married, in a sort of mock romance that no one takes seriously. This summer, Edna is the object of his attentions.

As Edna begins the process of identifying her true self, the self that exists apart from the identity she maintains as a wife and mother, Robert unknowingly encourages her by indulging her emerging sensuality. Unexpectedly, Robert and Edna become intensely infatuated with each other by summer's end. The sudden seriousness of his romantic feelings for her compels him to follow through on his oft-stated intention to go to Mexico to seek his fortune.

Edna is distraught at his departure, remaining obsessed with him long after she and her family have returned to New Orleans. As a result of her continuing process of self-discovery, she becomes almost capricious in meeting her desires and needs, no longer putting appearances first. Always interested in art, she begins spending more time painting and sketching portraits than on household and social duties. Léonce is shocked by Edna's refusal to obey social conventions. He consults Dr. Mandelet, an old family friend, who advises Léonce to leave Edna alone and allow her to get this odd behavior out of her system.

Edna continues her friendships with Mademoiselle Reisz and the pregnant Madame Ratignolle. Mademoiselle Reisz receives letters from Robert, which she allows Edna to read. Meanwhile, as a result of her awakening sexuality Edna has an affair with Alcée Arobin, a notorious womanizer. Her heart remains with Robert, however, and she is delighted to learn that he is soon returning to New Orleans.

She has grown ever more distant from Léonce, and also become a much better artist, selling some of her work through her art teacher. These sales provide her a small income, so while Léonce and the children are out of town, she decides to move out of the mansion they share and into a tiny rental house nearby, called the "pigeon house" for its small size.

Much to her distress, she encounters Robert accidentally, when he comes to visit Mademoiselle Reisz while Edna happens to be there. She is hurt that he did not seek her out as soon as he returned. Over the next weeks he tries to maintain emotional and physical distance from Edna because she is a married woman, but she ultimately forces the issue by kissing him, and he confesses his love to her.

Edna tries to express to Robert that she is utterly indifferent to the social prohibitions that forbid their love; she feels herself to be an independent woman. Before she can explain herself, however, she is called away to attend Madame Ratignolle's labor and delivery, at the end of which Madame Ratignolle asks Edna to consider the effect of her adulterous actions on her children. Edna is greatly disturbed to realize that her little boys will be deeply hurt if she leaves Léonce for another man. To this point, she had considered only her own desires.

When she returns to the pigeon house, Robert is gone, having left a goodbye note. Crushed, she decides to kill herself, realizing that she cannot return to her former life with Léonce but is also unwilling to hurt her children personally or socially with the stigma of divorce or open adultery. The next morning she travels alone to Grand Isle, announces that she is going swimming, and drowns herself.

List of Characters

Edna Pontellier Main protagonist who, while in a passionless marriage to Léonce Pontellier, falls in love with Robert Lebrun and has a brief affair with Alcée Arobin. A member of New Orleans' upper class, she has artistic leanings.

Léonce Pontellier Edna's husband, a successful and materialistic businessman.

Robert Lebrun Charismatic young man who falls in love with Edna during her summer on Grand Isle; has a history of maintaining mock romances with unattainable women.

Alcée Arobin Accomplished ladies' man who pursues an affair with Edna.

Mademoiselle Reisz   Virtuoso pianist whom Edna meets on Grand Isle. Upon returning to New Orleans, Edna visits her to hear her play piano and read letters that Robert has written to her.

Madame Adèle Ratignolle   The epitome of the "mother-woman," a devoted wife and mother whom Edna befriends on Grande Isle; their friendship continues while back in New Orleans.

Monsieur Ratignolle   Madame Ratignolle's husband, a successful pharmacist.

Madame Lebrun   Owner and hostess of the Grand Isle boardinghouse (called a *pension*); mother of Robert and Victor.

Victor Lebrun   Temperamental, strong-willed, and spoiled but very good-looking son of Madame Lebrun.

Mariequita   Flirtatious Spanish girl who has a crush on Victor and possibly on Robert, as well.

Etienne and Raoul Pontellier   Edna and Léonce's young sons.

The quadroon   Nanny to Edna's children.

Dr. Mandelet   Old family friend and physician to the Pontelliers, whom Léonce consults about Edna's strange behavior. The doctor knows but does not tell Léonce that Edna is in love with another man.

Mrs. James Highcamp   Middle-aged society woman who enjoys the company of fashionable young men; spends time at the racetrack with Edna and Alcée.

Mrs. Merriman   Friend of Mrs. Highcamp and Arobin; Edna comes into contact with Arobin through Mrs. Merriman and Mrs. Highcamp.

The Colonel   Edna's father, a retired colonel in the Confederate army.

Janet   Edna's younger sister, whose wedding Edna refuses to attend because of her distaste for marriage.

Margaret   Edna' older sister, who raised Edna after their mother died.

The lady in black   Highly devout, elderly woman staying at the Grand Isle boardinghouse, usually seen with a prayerbook or rosary in hand.

The lovers   Courting couple on Grand Isle usually seen by themselves, enthralled in their new romance.

Monsieur Farival   Elderly gentleman vacationing on Grand Isle at the boardinghouse.

The Farival twins   Monsieur Farival's granddaughters who repeatedly practice on piano a duet from the opera *Zampa*.

Celestine   Edna's live-in servant at the "pigeon house."

Laidpore   Edna's drawing teacher and art broker; he sells her work, allowing her a small income.

Montel   Old family friend of the Lebruns' whom Robert meets with in Mexico to seek his fortune.

Character Map

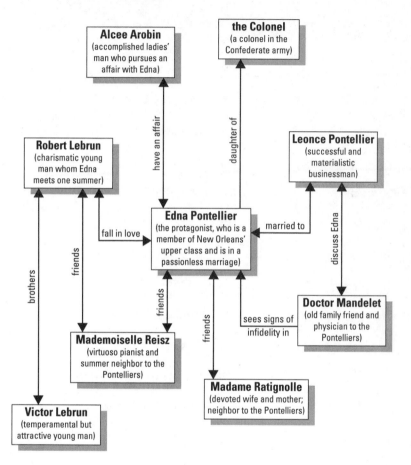

CRITICAL COMMENTARIES

Chapter I

Summary

The novel opens with Léonce Pontellier, a vacationer on Grand Isle (which is just off the coast of New Orleans), reading a newspaper and surveying his surroundings. He is annoyed by a caged parrot loudly repeating its stock phrases, and so leaves the main building of the *pension* (boardinghouse) for his own cottage. Léonce's wife, Edna Pontellier, and her friend Robert Lebrun return from their swim in the Gulf of Mexico and join Léonce. He soon departs for billiards and socializing at the nearby Klein's hotel.

Commentary

Already Chopin establishes some key symbolism in the novel: Edna is the green-and-yellow parrot telling everyone to "go away, for God's sake." Unable to leave the cage, the parrot must ask everyone to leave when it would prefer to simply fly away.

The parrot knows not only French, Spanish, and English phrases but also "a language which nobody understood, unless it was the mockingbird that hung on the other side of the door." The mockingbird represents Madame Reisz (a character who is introduced in Chapter IX), the only character who is successful at making Edna tell the truth about her love for Robert that develops throughout the novel. Later chapters show how Madame Reisz's piano playing speaks to Edna's soul as if that music were the language her soul had been waiting in silence for. Mockingbirds have a reputation as obnoxious birds, and Madame Reisz shares a similar reputation as a rude, ill-tempered woman. The description of the mockingbird also sets the tone for Madame Reisz's independent behavior within the confines of the insistently polite upper-class Creole society; she too whistles her own tune "with maddening persistence."

Character Insight

The nature of Edna's relationships with Léonce and Robert is established in this first brief chapter, as well. Léonce, noting his wife's sunburn, expresses not concern for her potential discomfort but instead regards her "as one looks at a valuable piece of personal property that has suffered some damage." Yet Léonce and Edna have built between them a working familiarity that allows them to communicate wordlessly, such as when he hands her rings to her at her simple wordless gesture of holding out her hand. Such nonverbal communication is a tremendous bond between a couple, and is often an indication of their unity.

At the same time, Edna clearly has a bond with her platonic friend Robert that excludes her husband—this bond is represented by the adventure that she and Robert share during their swim, the joy of which they cannot communicate to Léonce. While Léonce is familiar, Robert is fun and lively. At 26, he is only two years younger than Edna, while Léonce is 12 years older. Ironically Léonce is clearly not threatened by Robert's friendship with his wife: When Robert declines Léonce's invitation to accompany him to Klein's hotel, stating "quite frankly that he preferred to . . . talk to Mrs. Pontellier," Léonce simply tells Edna to "send him about his business when he bores you."

Literary Device

Another motif set up in this chapter is the significance of music in Edna's life and in the novel. Two twin girls, children of other vacationers at the *pension*, can be heard practicing a piano duet from an opera in which a character drowns at sea—foreshadowing musically Edna's ultimate fate.

Issue of class and race are implicitly addressed, as well: Edna's own children have a quadroon (meaning she is one-quarter African) nanny. She attends to Edna's boys "with a faraway, meditative air." However, while she may be entertaining the same thoughts of independence from society's demands that Edna later has, she lacks the economic freedom to pursue life on her own terms, particularly in the intensely bigoted atmosphere of 1890s Louisiana. Like most of the servant characters, she is not named and her voice is never heard.

Glossary

(Here and in the following sections, difficult words and phrases are explained.)

"Allez vous-en! Sapristi!"   French phrases meaning "Go away! For God's sake!"

Grand Isle   an island off the Louisiana coast, about fifty miles south of New Orleans.

Zampa   an opera written by Ferdinand Herold in which a character drowns at sea.

telling her beads   praying on her rosary.

pension   a term used in France and other continental countries for a boardinghouse.

Chênière Caminada   a small island lying between Grand Isle and the Louisiana coast.

lugger   a small vessel equipped with a lugsail or lugsails.

quadroon   a person who has one black grandparent; child of a mulatto and a white.

sunshade   a parasol used for protection against the sun's rays.

lawn sleeves   sleeves made from lawn, a fine, sheer cloth of linen or cotton.

Chapter II

Summary

As Edna and Robert continue chatting on the porch of the Pontelliers' cottage, they reveal more of their backgrounds and personalities. Robert has long had youthful intentions of going to Mexico to seek his fortune but has yet to follow through and so remains at his modest job in his native New Orleans. Edna speaks of her family and their homes in Mississippi and Kentucky. Then, while Edna gets ready for dinner, Robert plays with her two young boys.

Commentary

Edna's physical description seems to provide insight into her character: "Her face was captivating by reason of a certain frankness of expression and a contradictory subtle play of features." Contradiction and frankness underlie her imminent rejection of the society that she comes to feel is imprisoning her.

Chopin describes Edna with the potent phrase "She was an American woman"—an identity that differentiates her from the Creoles around her, who maintain multilingual ties to their French and Spanish heritage. In contrast, Edna's French background was "lost in dilution." The term "American woman" evokes all the qualities that stereotypically characterize Americans: independence, boldness, and a desire to conquer new territory. Yet those qualities were not welcome in American women of the 1890s, when women—particularly those of the leisure class to which Edna belongs—were rewarded for passivity, dependence, and staying at home.

While, as a man, Robert is free to seek his fortune in Mexico, he has not yet followed through on this frequently stated intention. Instead, he has always "held on to his modest position in a mercantile house," seemingly content to keep hold of a safe job within his native city and spend summers with his mother. His youth and inexperience are highlighted in this chapter; Chopin describes him as talking much about himself because "He was very young, and did not know any better." At the same time, Edna "talked a little about herself for the same reason." Their relationship seems based more on harmless mutual entertainment than on an emotional or intellectual connection. Rather than discussing any topic with depth or insight, they instead "chatted incessantly," a phrase that brings to mind a couple of schoolgirls rather than a pair of potential lovers. The lack of depth in their relationship at this point may indicate a falsity at the root of their later passion.

Glossary

countenance   the look on a person's face that shows one's nature or feelings.

"The Poet and the Peasant"   an operetta by Franz von Suppé (1819–1895), Austrian conductor and composer of popular operettas.

Quartier Français   rench Quarter, also known as the Old Quarter; the oldest part of New Orleans and the area in which most New Orleans' Creoles lived.

Chapter III

Summary

That night when Léonce returns from Klein's hotel, cheerful and talkative, Edna is already asleep. His entrance wakes her and he tries to elicit responses to his gossip despite her sleepiness. Checking on the sleeping boys, he reports to Edna that Raoul has a fever and compels her to check on the boy, despite her objections that Raoul was quite healthy when he went to bed. By the time Léonce goes to sleep, Edna is fully awake. She goes onto the porch and cries until the mosquitoes force her back inside to bed.

The next morning, Léonce leaves for New Orleans for the work-week. He sends a box of sweet and savory treats to Edna, which she shares with everyone else at Grand Isle.

Commentary

Léonce's behavior upon returning home illustrates his perception of his wife as more of an amusement than a partner. When he arrives home, possibly drunk (considering his exuberant and talkative mood), he awakens Edna from a sound sleep but expects her to chatter back at him. He is displeased that "his wife . . . evinced so little interest in things which concerned him, and valued so little his conversation." In later chapters, contrast this insensitivity and selfishness on Léonce's part with the studied courtliness and chivalry displayed by Arobin and Robert.

Not only does Léonce awaken her to provide an audience for his anecdotes, he also chastises her for not immediately checking on the fever that he mistakenly perceives in Raoul. When, instead, she asserts that Raoul likely does not have a fever because he gave no sign of sickness up until he went to bed, Léonce accuses her of neglecting the children. His reproach, voiced "in a monotonous, insistent way," is ostensibly sensible, given that they have divided up the family support duties, with Léonce working outside the home in a brokerage business while Edna assumes full responsibility for all domestic areas, including childcare. Yet this division of labor was not the option actively selected by Edna but the default choice of her society and culture. While Léonce can anticipate on Sundays the upcoming "lively week on Carondelet Street," Edna remains another week on Grand Isle, limited to the few pursuits available to children and the other mothers. With the lively Robert as her greatest diversion, perhaps her infatuation with him is inevitable.

By the time Edna establishes that Raoul does not have a fever—evidenced in how quickly she returns to their bedroom—Edna is "thoroughly awake" while Léonce is soon "fast asleep," unable to apologize for his accusations. This incident sparks a bout of crying; Edna takes her tears onto the front porch. At this point Edna is herself not sure why she is crying, because similar occurrences of her husband's rudeness and insensitivity "were not uncommon in her married life." Previously, she had mentally weighed such incidences against Léonce's ostensible kindness, such as the box of bonbons and patés he soon sends her from New Orleans. Chopin indicates that Edna has not yet reached any kind of palpable resistance to her husband and the submissive role her asks her to play: "She did not sit there inwardly upbraiding her husband, lamenting at Fate. . . . She was just having a good cry all to herself." This "good cry" precludes the dissatisfaction with her married life that develops in later chapters.

Literary Device

Note that Edna is prevented from having a full-on romantic brooding on the porch by the mosquitoes attacking her arms—a realistic consideration in what could have become a dramatic sulk.

Léonce must feel he can buy favor with money: When Edna counts out the dollar bills she'll use to buy her sister a wedding present, Léonce objects "Oh! We'll treat Sister Janet better than that." Because he didn't treat his wife very well the night before but sends her bonbons later, he clearly equates material gifts as a substitute for kindness and sensitivity. When Edna shares the box of goodies with the others, everyone declares that Léonce "was the best husband in the world" for his material gesture. In response Edna "was forced to admit that she knew of none better" but the value of such an admission is doubtful when it is forced. The seeds of disenchantment with her husband—and by extension, her life—have been planted and are just beginning to consider sprouting.

Glossary

consuming   wasting away; perishing.

peignoir   a woman's loose, full dressing gown; like a negligee.

mules   lounging slippers that do not cover the heels.

rockaway   a light horse-drawn carriage with four wheels, open sides, and a standing top.

Carondelet Street   the center of New Orleans' financial district.

friandises   delicacies.

pâtés   meat pies.

Chapter IV

Summary

Madame Ratignolle is introduced in this chapter as the embodiment of the "mother-women," the Creole wives who always place husband and children before themselves. Because Edna's behavior and attitudes differ from the mother-women's, Léonce sometimes doubts Edna's devotion to her children. Madame Ratignolle, sewing winter garments for her children, openly makes references to her pregnancy, which shocks Edna who is taken aback by mention of any matter pertaining to sex. Edna finds that Creole women do not share such taboos and are more open to discussion and literature containing references to sexual matters.

Commentary

The key development in this chapter is the distinction Chopin makes between Edna and the mother-women, those women who, nun-like, "esteemed it a holy privilege to efface themselves as individuals and grow wings as ministering angels." Such winged angels are quite different from the birds described in Chapter I—the anti-social parrot and the obnoxious mockingbird that represent Edna and Madame Reisz. The mother-women idolize their children and husbands, feeling it appropriate and necessary to sacrifice their own personal needs and expression.

Madame Ratignolle is described as "the embodiment of every womanly grace and charm," the ultimate mother-woman. Despite their philosophical differences, Madame Ratignolle greatly enjoys Edna's company, possibly because Edna is the only non-Creole among the Grand Isle vacationers and so provides more diversion. At this point, Edna is still following social conventions faithfully: Although she thinks it excessive of Madame Ratignolle to make winter clothes for her children during the summer, Edna dutifully copies the sewing pattern for later use so that she will not appear "unamiable and uninterested."

Chopin's description of the all-enclosing winter pajamas lends a hysterical tone to their construction: The pajamas are meant to protect the child from "insidious currents of deadly cold" that may find "their way through keyholes." Edna feels her children's summer needs are being met and isn't interested in anticipating their winter needs, a pragmatic approach that probably underlies Léonce's doubts about Edna's devotion to her children—she is not inclined to become hysterical about their welfare. Her children seem to have benefited from her calmness: When they take a spill during playtime, each boy is likely to "pick himself up . . . and go on playing" rather than rush to his mother. In fact, in playground conflicts, Edna's boys "usually prevailed against the other mother-tots" who are more dependent upon their mothers as external sources of comfort and strength.

Note that Léonce and Robert were probably raised by mother-women, in contrast to Edna, who lost her mother at an early age. Robert, in fact, continues to return to his mother during summers, an extension of little mother-tots' tendency to run to their mothers.

Another way in which Edna differs from the Creole women is, ironically, her prudery. Mainstream America in the 1890s considered taboo any aspect of life that touched upon sex, such as pregnancy and childbirth. In contrast, Creole women openly share their reproductive experiences with the men and feel no prohibition against reading novels with erotic content. Their ability to discuss such matters does not extend to their behavior: The Creole women seemed to have an innate "lofty chastity," an assurance that perhaps makes it possible for them to make references to sexual matters, confident in their virtue.

Edna is shocked by their free speech and blushes when Robert makes reference to one woman's pregnancy—such extreme modesty in speech now contrasts markedly with her behavior later as she rejects the very essence of her role in society.

Glossary

"condition"   here, the condition of being pregnant.

Creole   a person descended from the original French settlers of Louisiana, especially of the New Orleans area.

accouchement   childbirth.

Chapter V

Summary

As Madame Ratignolle sews the children's winter garments, Edna sketches her and chats with Robert. After Edna has completed the sketch, Madame Ratignolle claims to feel a fainting spell coming on; Edna and Robert quickly respond by fanning her and spritzing her with cologne. Recovering speedily, Madame Ratignolle returns to her cottage, and Robert compels Edna to go for their daily swim.

Commentary

This chapter reveals Robert's history as a sort of harmless womanizer. Although he seems to court a new woman each summer, his courtship is all form and no content. Chopin describes Creole husbands as passionless; Robert's supposed passion as a young single man similarly is without substance. Although he and Edna spend a great deal of time together, no one (not even Edna) is suspicious of their relationship or of Robert's intentions. When he lays his head on her arm while she is sketching, she "could not but believe it to be thoughtlessness on his part; yet that was no reason she should submit to it." So far, his devotion to Edna has not been framed in mock romance, for which she is grateful. "It would have been unacceptable and annoying" to her. At this point, Edna retains her allegiance to the morality of her culture.

Character
Insight

At the same time, however, Edna has a susceptibility to sensuality that is inevitably linked to romance, to the soft touch of the warm breeze and the swim that Robert promises to be "delicious." At Robert's insistence that she go for a swim with him, Edna hears the Gulf's "sonorous murmur . . . like a loving but imperative entreaty"—echoing Robert's "murmured" words of spurned love earlier in the chapter. Robert is coming to represent sensuality and passion for her: He invites her to sensual experiences and uses sensual language.

Engaging with the sensuous world partly motivates her enjoyment of drawing, a hobby that gives her "satisfaction of a kind which no other employment afforded her," including motherhood. She can't resist sketching Madame Ratignolle because she appears in the light of sunset as a "sensuous Madonna"—the second reference to Madame Ratignolle as a Madonna in the chapter.

Theme

Such a designation possibly indicates the unattainability of all that Madame Ratignolle represents. Further, because Edna was not raised Catholic (a religion that places a great deal of importance on the Virgin Mary), her view of the Madonna is from the perspective of an outsider—one who was not brought up to value a supreme mother figure.

Edna herself is no Madonna: When her children appear on the porch, she "sought to detain them for a little talk and some pleasantry" as if they were social callers rather than her small boys. In contrast, Madame Ratignolle showers her clingy children with "a thousand endearments" while cuddling the smallest in her arms. Note that immediately prior to complaining of feeling faint, she neatly collects her sewing work and supplies, rolls it all together and pins it "securely"— hardly the behavior of someone feeling faint. Madame Ratignolle takes advantage of her society's view of woman as helpless to exert a kind of power over others, power she cannot exert directly while still remaining within her culture's bounds of propriety.

Glossary

Daudet   Alphonse Daudet (1840–1897), a French novelist of the naturalist school.

camaraderie   loyalty and warm, friendly feeling among comrades; comradeship.

passez! adieu! allez vous-en!   Go on! Good-bye! Go away!

blaguer! farceur! grose bête, va!   Comedian! Clown! Silly beast, away with you!

mais ce n'est pas mal! elle s'y connait, elle a de la force, oui   But that's not bad at all! She knows what she's doing, she has a talent.

cologne water   eau de cologne.

Chapter VI

Summary

This purely expository chapter clearly foreshadows Edna's death and establishes its cause as the process of self-discovery which she has just begun, a process facilitated by her contact with the warm Gulf waters. She is starting to understand the limitations of and feel constrained by the expectations of her culture.

Commentary

This chapter establishes Edna's relationship to the sea and its role as a catalyst in her awakening to herself, her needs, and her desires. Edna is beginning to see a "certain light . . . the light which, showing the way, forbids it." While in the previous chapter she resented Robert's head on her arm, the resentment may have sprung from the recognition that she could not respond in kind, not free to explore the parameters of passion that Robert affects—passion that her husband doesn't pretend to possess. The sea, where she swims with Robert, appeals to and awakens her innate sensuality. The warm waters of the Gulf of Mexico are "sensuous, enfolding the body in its soft, close embrace" much as a lover would, but also as the muffling touch of death. The water's seductive voice compels Edna's soul to "lose itself in mazes of inward contemplation," a symbol of how her burgeoning interest in realizing her own desires and needs overcomes the maintenance of her life as she knew it, ultimately taking her very life itself.

Literary Device

Note that Chopin repeats sentences from the final two paragraphs of this chapter in the novel's final chapter, when she describes Edna's fatal swim.

Glossary

vouchsafe   to be gracious enough or condescend to give or grant.

Chapters VII and VIII

Summary

In Chapter VII, Edna and Madame Ratignolle walk to the beach and sit on the porch of their adjoining beach houses. Edna confides to Madame Ratignolle much of her past history of infatuation with unattainable men. They are interrupted by Robert approaching with their children. Edna joins the children in their play tent on the beach while Madame Ratignolle asks Robert to help her back to her cottage.

In Chapter VIII, Madame Ratignolle asks Robert to leave Edna alone rather than continue with his devoted, if platonic, attentions. He takes offense, pointing out that he is not like Alcée Arobin, a well-known womanizer. After walking Madame Ratignolle to her room, Robert joins his mother, who mentions that their friend Montel is in Mexico, should Robert like to join him there to pursue business interests. Robert is impatient to learn more about this prospect but is easily distracted by his mother's mention of Edna's likely return from the beach.

Commentary

Character Insight

Chapter VII reveals much about Edna's history of rebellion: running away into the fields to escape her father's gloomy prayer services and marrying Léonce not out of personal passion for him but because of her family's "violent opposition" to her marrying a Catholic man. All her life she has maintained the duality of "that outward existence which conforms, the inward life which questions." Even her physique differs from other women's; her body "occasionally fell into splendid poses," displaying a rather severe physical grace that sets her apart from other women. Note, however, that Chopin uses the term "occasionally" rather than "consistently:" Edna's small life is not one destined for greatness.

Prior to her married life, Edna experienced several sexual, passionate obsessions with men that could not lead to actual relationships. While fixated on a dead writer, Edna felt that the "persistence of the infatuation lent it an aspect of genuineness. The hopelessness of it colored it with the lofty tones of a great passion." Such a perception of passion for a dead man, whom she never met, indicates the severity of Edna's weakness for the melodrama of unrequited or unfulfilled love. Further, she enjoyed the subterfuge of such a relationship: "Anyone may possess the portrait of a tragedian without exciting suspicion or comment. (This was a sinister reflection which she cherished.)" Her infatuations may seem grand in their intensity of feeling but are actually rather childish in scope. When she says about her running away from the prayer services that "I was a little unthinking child . . . just following a misleading impulse without question," she could be describing her entire life—the small-scale romantic obsessions, her marriage to Léonce, having her own children. Even her actions later in the novel arise partly from genuine rebellion and partly from whimsy.

As she confides many of these things to Madame Ratignolle, she experiences for the first time a genuine expression of her small self, which intoxicates her "like wine, or like a first breath of freedom." Relating her history of minor rebellions and hopeless passions, she sets the stage for her development that summer into the kind of woman who is strong enough to act on her dissatisfaction with her role as wife and mother that is so far from her true personality, which craves independence.

Significantly, she tells Madame Ratignolle "sometimes I feel this summer as if I were walking through the green meadows again; idly, aimlessly, unthinking and unguided." Not only does this description foreshadow her death in water that reminds her of waves of grass, but also indicates that Edna is once again "running away from prayers," turning her back on the values of organized religion and her own culture.

Note that Edna realizes with relief after she is married that "no trace of passion . . . colored her affection [for Léonce], thereby threatening its dissolution." Ironically, her lack of passion for her husband drives her to Robert, who attempts to portray himself as a grandly passionate man. Further, if all passion eventually burns itself out, so too will her love for Robert, a fact she realizes in the end.

While Chapter VII depicts Madame Ratignolle as not much of a thinker (she objects when Edna becomes momentarily analytical), Chapter VIII reveals her as a shrewd realist about interpersonal dynamics, asking Robert to "let Mrs. Pontellier alone." Having heard Edna's confession of past infatuations, Madame Ratignolle is attempting to short circuit the likely development of an attachment that can cause only marital and social conflict.

Robert's response certainly foreshadows his ultimate entanglement with Edna. Although he has established a pattern of engaging in rhetoric instead of action—the mock romances with married women, the unfulfilled intention to seek his fortune in Mexico—evidently he does wish to be taken seriously, to receive credit as a passionate lover and successful entrepreneur based on his intentions rather than his acts. "I hope she has discernment enough to find in me something besides the *blaguer*," he says, revealing the attitude that Edna could only do herself credit to find worth in him and perceive him as a man to be reckoned with. Yet Madame Ratignolle immediately and candidly identifies the truth of the situation: "You speak with about as little reflection as . . . one of those children down there." Robert is still emotionally immature, which probably motivates his hollow romantic gestures towards women with whom he never expects to pursue a serious adult relationship.

Note that Robert offers as proof of his own virtue a comparison to Alcée Arobin, the gentleman with whom Edna will become sexually involved later.

Although he initially resents Madame Ratignolle's suggestion, betraying his own illusions about the depth of his character, by the time they reach her cottage, he has regained enough composure to admit that Madame Ratignolle should have instead "warned me against taking myself seriously. Your advice might then have . . . given me subject for some reflection." However, if Madame Ratignolle's comment does cause him to engage in reflection, it is more likely speculation about the situation's possibilities, as is implied by how easily he is distracted from Montel's letter by the suggestion that Edna may be approaching. Madame Ratignolle's well-meant advice underlies Robert and Edna's later emotional entanglement, poised as both are, like children, to indulge in the high drama of thwarted romance.

The ideal of romance is illustrated by the courting couple who is also vacationing at the *pension*, shown "leaning toward each other as the wateroaks bent from the sea. There was not a particle on earth beneath their feet," so high are they on the newness and passion of their romance. Interestingly, the sternly religious lady in black is frequently shown "creeping behind them," like a dark cloud threatening their happiness. The lady in black represents anti-passion: She moves slowly, is always alone, and is usually engaged in religious rituals such as praying on her rosary. She is the cooling of passion that inevitably follows the first flush of romance and youth's energetic infatuations.

Representing the sometimes-negative energy of youth is Victor, Robert's younger brother. Victor's impetuous, willful behavior indicates a lack of consideration for others, a trait often tempered by the responsibilities and realities of adult life. While Robert does not have his younger brother's temper, his habit of spending summers at his mother's resort paying court to married women rather than pursuing a career or a wife renders his own level of emotional maturity suspect.

Glossary

fashion-plate   a fashionably dressed person.

muslin   any of various strong, often sheer cotton fabrics of plain weave; especially a heavy variety used for sheets, pillowcases, and so on.

collar   a cloth band or folded-over piece attached to the neck of a garment.

gallery   a veranda or porch.

crash   a coarse cotton or linen cloth with a plain, loose weave, used for towels, curtains, clothes, and so on.

lateen   a triangular, fore-and-aft-rigged sail suspended on a slant from a portion of the ship's mast.

ma chère   my dear.

pauvre chérie   poor dear.

held controversies   conducted a lengthy discussion of an important question in which opposing opinions clash.

Tiens! Voilà que Madame Ratignolle est jalouse!   Finally! It appears that Madame Ratignolle is jealous!

programme   the acts, speeches, and musical pieces that make up an entertainment or ceremony.

Ma foi!   Indeed! (literally "my goodness").

au revoir   goodbye.

bouillon   a clear broth, usually of beef.

Sèvres   a type of fine French porcelain.

bon garçon   good boy (or good waiter).

ether   the upper regions of space; clear sky.

treadle   a lever or pedal moved by the foot as to turn a wheel.

Goncourt   Edmond Louis Antoine Huot de Goncourt (1822–1896); French novelist and art critic.

tête montée   hot-headed person.

Chapters IX, X, and XI

Summary

After dinner one Saturday night, the vacationers attend an impromptu children's musical recital, and the adults dance to Madame Ratignolle's piano playing. Robert tells Edna that Mademoiselle Reisz will perform a piece at Edna's request. Although Mademoiselle Reisz is generally bad-tempered and unwilling to freely display her talents, she agrees to perform because she likes Edna (yet dislikes all the other guests). Edna is deeply shaken by Mademoiselle Reisz's performance, experiencing viscerally the emotions of the piece. Mademoiselle Reisz is pleased by Edna's involved, tearful response. Then, at Robert's suggestion, everyone sets out for a late-night swim.

In Chapter X, as the group makes its way to the beach, Edna reflects that Robert seems to be avoiding her lately. At the beach, Edna truly swims for the first time, rather than splashing in the shallows. After her ambitious swim, during which she goes farther from shore than she feels is safe, she abruptly leaves for her cottage. Robert accompanies her and sits on the porch, while she settles in the porch hammock. They feel the first stirrings of desire for each other.

In Chapter XI, Edna refuses to leave the hammock and join Léonce inside the cottage at his return, insisting that she is comfortable in the hammock. Although initially irritated, he handles the situation calmly by joining her on the porch. When she goes inside to sleep, just before dawn, Léonce remains on the porch to finish his cigar.

Commentary

Style & Language

This chapter's opening description of the party lamps also indicates ideal party parameters: "every lamp turned as high as it could be without smoking the chimney or threatening explosion." This description could apply as well to the romantic relations considered ideal by Edna's culture. While the flame of passion may be burning brightly, it should not become so hot as to cause behavior that threatens the monogamous, Catholic values of their culture or besmirch anyone's good reputation with scandal—the social equivalents of smoking the chimney or causing explosions.

The emphasis on good behavior continues as the Farival twins yet again play the musical pieces they've been playing all summer. The parrot seems to object to hearing these pieces repeated, loudly uttering his stock phrase in French "Go away, for God's sake!" The twins' grandfather is angry at this apparent candor and lobbies to have the bird removed. Such punishment for honesty foreshadows the negative reaction Edna will invoke when she starts telling the truth about her dissatisfaction with her life.

Chapter IX contrasts Madame Ratignolle with Mademoiselle Reisz. Both play piano, but Madame Ratignolle plays as "a means of brightening the home and making it attractive." Playing competently and with spirit, her performances serve only to make her even more attractive than she already is. In stark contrast, Mademoiselle Reisz is disliked by and dislikes almost everyone, lacking interpersonal skills, fashion sense, and physical attractiveness. Yet her performance is that of a master, stirring everyone within earshot with the power of music. Edna is particularly affected by the music, which "sent a keen tremor" down her spine. Note the connection between music and the sea: "the very passions themselves were aroused within her soul, swaying it, lashing it, as the waves daily beat upon her splendid body." Like the warm Gulf waters, music appeals to Edna's inclination to indulge in the drama of high feeling. Her visceral reaction is an indication of her awakening desire to experience some great passion in her life; "her being was tempered to take an impress of the abiding truth" for the first time.

In Chapter X, the mock romance Robert has been indulging in with Edna begins to assume a genuine air. In response to Madame Ratignolle's advice, he has been avoiding Edna some days, causing her to miss him "just as one misses the sun on a cloudy day without having thought much about the sun when it was shining"—hardly a passionate state to begin with.

Yet Edna experiences in Chapter X a breakthrough in her ability to swim, which symbolizes the blossoming of her desire to leave behind social constraints, "to swim far out, where no woman had swum before." As she realizes the ease with which she can power herself through the water, "She grew daring and reckless, overestimating her strength." Of course she will engage in such daring later as she begins to flout convention and obey her own desires.

After her initial bold progress into the Gulf, she soon finds that she has swum farther out than she can actually swim back—she has made more progress than she can handle. Again her death is foreshadowed when she is struck by "a quick vision of death" that terrifies her. Léonce fails to appreciate her terror, pointing out that "I was watching you" as if his placid observation from shore could prevent her from drowning, or from later having an affair with Alcée Arobin.

Character Insight

Edna's childlike aspect is emphasized in the description of her as a "little tottering, stumbling, clutching child, who of a sudden realizes its powers, and walks for the first time alone, boldly and with over-confidence." Of course, this description applies to not only learning to swim but also to her actions later in the novel when she feels the power of refusing to follow certain social conventions.

Chapter X ends with the beginning of Edna's deeper entanglement with Robert. When he tells her the tale of the Gulf spirit whom she has captivated, he is also referring to himself. After the powerful music and the liberating swim, Edna is primed for further emotional stimulation and Robert is there to further his romantic interests with the one woman who may take him seriously in that regard.

Chapter XI demonstrates Edna's potential for defiance. While Edna's wish to remain in the hammock begins as a caprice, it assumes the character of rebellion after Léonce orders her to come inside. Continuing the portrayal of Edna as childlike, Léonce waits out her display of rebellion as though she is a toddler in the midst of a tantrum. When she insists that she will remain in the hammock as long as she likes, his response is calm and methodical: drinking a glass of wine, offering one to Edna, joining her on the porch, and placing his feet up on the railing. His cigar-smoking presence is stifling to Edna's rebellious mood. In fact, he outdoes her when he remains on the porch after she herself yields to the physical need for sleep and goes inside to bed. As the night begins to edge toward dawn, thwarted by Léonce's smug presence on the porch, she "began to feel like one who awakens gradually out of a . . . delicious, grotesque, impossible dream . . . the exuberance . . . yielding to the conditions which crowded her in." As with the swim in the previous chapter, she is delighted to experience a sense of autonomy, which unfortunately dissolves when she tests its limits. These small defeats indicate her greatest weakness: Edna's spirit is strong enough to begin a rebellion but too weak to maintain it.

Glossary

dedicated to the Blessed Virgin committed by their parents at birth to become nuns.

Chopin [Frédéric] François Chopin (1810–1849); Polish composer and pianist, lived in France after 1831.

Bon Dieu Good God.

pathos the quality in something experienced or observed that arouses feelings of pity, sorrow, sympathy, or compassion.

repose to lie at rest.

grotesque ludicrously eccentric or strange; ridiculous; absurd.

Chapters XII, XIII, and XIV

Summary

After a brief and fitful sleep, Edna awakens with an impulsive desire to attend church. She summons Robert to accompany her. On the ferry ride to the *Chênière*, Robert chats briefly with a Spanish girl named Mariequita, who relays gossip about a local Spanish man who runs away with another man's wife. Robert shushes her with some emotion, then becomes thoroughly involved in Edna's presence. They make plans to go to a small nearby island by themselves the next day for sightseeing. Having reached *Chênière*, they go to church.

Once in church, Edna feels stifled and drowsy. She leaves during the service, accompanied by Robert. He takes her to his friend Tonie's house, where Tonie's mother, Madame Antoine, puts Edna in the guestroom. Edna sleeps for several hours, till late afternoon. Robert fixes a meal for her while Madame Antoine is out. When Madame Antoine returns, they listen to her tell stories until after nightfall. Robert borrows Tonie's boat so that he and Edna can return to Grande Isle.

Upon returning to her cottage, Edna finds that her youngest child is too cranky to sleep. She rocks him to sleep and Robert helps her put the boy to bed before heading for the beach. Edna sits alone and considers her changing perspective on life. Missing Robert, she sings the song he sang to her on the trip back "*si tu savais*" ("if you knew").

Commentary

The morning after her swim, Edna is still haunted by a sense of the "delicious, grotesque, impossible dream" of the previous night. During her brief sleep, she had dreams that she cannot remember after awakening, leaving her with the feeling of pursuing the unattainable. This morning she is a changed person, "blindly following whatever impulse moved her, as if she had . . . freed her soul of responsibility" during the heady events of the previous night.

Her first impulsive act of the day is to send for Robert so that he can accompany her to *Chênière*. This impulse is significant, because she had never requested his presence before. When he meets her, "his face was suffused with a quiet glow," indicating that he is aware of and pleased by the new tone their relationship has assumed.

His brief conversation with Mariequita is telling of his honed sensitivity to the situation. When he assures Mariequita that Edna cannot be his "sweetheart" because she is married with children, Mariequita responds matter-of-factly with local gossip about a man who ran off with another man's wife and child. Her tale indicates that such things are possible, which causes him to reply "Shut up!" with uncharacteristic rudeness, as if he is suddenly uncomfortable with the potential turn his relationship with Edna may take.

Mariequita represents an open sexuality, with her tales of forbidden love and her flirting with Robert and Beaudelet. When Robert begins ignoring her in favor of Edna, she regards him with "childish ill humor and reproach," again connecting childishness and sensuality.

Note that when Mariequita inquires whether the young lovers are married, Robert laughs when he replies, "Of course not." For such passion to occur within the stable (and adult) institution of marriage seems unthinkable to him. This attitude echoes Edna's own feeling: Chapter VII reveals that Edna took "some unaccountable satisfaction that no trace of passion" was found in her marriage, "threatening its dissolution" with passion's instability or whimsy.

Whimsy underlies the growing connection between Edna and Robert. They plan to steal away by themselves to Grande Terre and find pirate treasure with the help of the Gulf spirit captivated by Edna—a distinctly romantic venture as evidenced by Robert's blushing face. Edna's insistence that they take the pirate gold and "throw it to the four winds, for the fun of seeing the golden specks fly" represents the ultimate devotion to capricious pleasure. Their conversation reveals that Edna has found a willing partner to indulge her love of sensuality.

Edna's overwhelming need in Chapter XIII to "quit the stifling atmosphere of the church and reach the open air" is symbolic of her increasing disinterest in meeting the demands of convention.

Note that as Edna and Robert make their way to Madame Antoine's, the text has a marked increase in visual and kinesthetic language, as if to contrast their day together away from their families with the soporific church or with the subculture left on Grand Isle. Chopin uses imagery more strongly now than previously in the novel to convey a sense of the *Chênière's* sensual appeal: "little gray, weather-beaten houses nestled peacefully among the orange trees," a fence "made of sea-drift," the "big four-posted bed, snow white" and holding the "sweet country odor of laurel."

As if inspired by the sensual island, after Edna has taken off most of her clothing for her nap, she runs her fingers through her hair and rubs her bare arms thoughtfully as if "for the first time" she realizes "the fine, firm quality and texture of her flesh." This new appreciation for her body follows the events of the previous night: the music that stirred wild passions in her heart, the liberation of swimming, the palpable desire experienced in Robert's presence.

Theme

Again childishness is linked with sensuality as Robert is "childishly gratified to discover her appetite" when she lustily devours the meal he prepared. Unlike Léonce, Robert appeals to Edna's imagination, her hunger for fantasy. He plays along with her suggestion that she had slept a hundred years and introduces her to Madame Antoine, who spins stories of adventure and treasure.

Literary Device

Edna is captivated by the environment that Robert introduces to her and fosters with his own stories. On the return trip to Grand Isle, she "could hear the whispering voices of dead men and the click of muffled gold"—the novel's most vividly descriptive language yet. Chopin thus depicts the growing appeal of all Robert represents to Edna.

Note, also, that twice in Chapter XIII Robert touches her clothing, such as when he plays with her skirt hem during the storytelling or "familiarly adjusted a ruffle upon her shoulder." While the contact alone is significant, also key is the air of familiarity—that quality being the greatest bond between Edna and her husband. Her relationship with Robert takes on an even more familiar air in Chapter XIV, when he assumes a husband's role in helping her put Etienne to bed. And just as the tone of their relationship has changed, so too has Edna changed, although by how much even she does not yet realize.

Character Insight

At the end of their day together, clearly Edna is falling in love, evidenced by her silent evaluation of Robert's voice as "not pretentious" but "musical and true"—as if she is comparing his voice to Léonce's more formal, pretentious personality.

Note that Etienne could not be soothed by Madame Ratignolle, the epitome of mother-women, but needed his mother's presence before he could be soothed to sleep. While Edna may not be the model mother in her husband's eyes, still her children have a necessary attachment that is unique to her. When at the end of the novel she considers the impact that her behavior will have on her children, this strong bond is uppermost in her mind.

Glossary

Grande Terre   a nearby island.

pirogue   a dugout canoe.

sea-drift   driftwood, wood drifting in the water, or that has been washed ashore.

Acadian   descendant of the French Canadians who in 1755 left Acadia, a former French colony (1604–1713) on the northeast coast of North America.

dispose   to arrange (matters); settle or regulate (affairs).

cover   a tablecloth and setting for a meal, especially for one person.

Vespers   the sixth of the seventh canonical hours; evening prayer.

Baratarians   natives of the Baratarian Islands, located off the Louisiana coast east of Caminada Bay and Grand Isle.

Chapter XV

Summary

Some days later, when Edna arrives in the dining hall for dinner, she is shocked to learn that Robert is leaving that night for Mexico. After dinner, she returns alone to her cottage, upset. Robert stops at her cottage on his way to the dock. Edna chastises him for his haste and secrecy; he offers no apology or excuse but asks her not to be angry with him. As he walks away, Edna realizes that she is in the midst of the same sort of obsessive infatuation she experienced in her youth.

Commentary

Robert's sudden departure reveals that he has begun falling in love with Edna. His overly formal goodbye; his blurted statement that he was looking forward to seeing her in New Orleans; and his sudden, secret resolve to leave attest to an emotional motivation for his trip.

His departure also provides a catalyst for Edna's realization that she is once again infatuated with an unobtainable man. Yet her past experiences "offered no lesson which she was willing to heed." Rather than recognizing that she is prone to falling in love with unattainable men now that she is the one who is unattainable, Edna focuses only on the loss of her current source of romance, the person who caters to her desire for imaginative and sensual living. Her conviction that "she had lost that which . . . her impassioned, newly awakened being demanded" arises in part from Robert's contribution to the formation of that self with his tall tales of spirits and pirate gold and swimming lessons in the sultry Gulf waters.

Note that when Edna returns to her cottage after dinner that night, she is unsuccessful at helping her boys fall asleep, but instead riles them even further with an unfinished bed time story. Her unrest over Robert negatively affects her parenting.

Glossary

Bedlam   any place or condition of noise and confusion.

court bouillon   an aromatic liquid used especially for poaching fish and made by cooking together white wine, water, onions, celery, carrots, and herbs.

indulgence   a partial or complete remission, under conditions specified by the Catholic church, of divine temporal punishment that may otherwise still be due for sin committed but forgiven.

close   here, confined or confining; narrow.

commodious   offering plenty of room; spacious; roomy.

Chapter XVI

Summary

After Robert's departure, Edna tries to assuage her longing for him by spending more time with Madame Lebrun and inducing others, including Léonce, into conversation about Robert. She experiences no guilt about her feelings for Robert—or about getting her husband to talk about him—because she feels she is entitled to a private emotional life, a hidden self. Edna reveals her idea of the self in a conversation with Madame Ratignolle, insisting that although she would give her life for her children, she would not sacrifice her self, a distinction that Madame Ratignolle fails to grasp.

On her way to the beach for a swim, Edna encounters Mademoiselle Reisz, who tells her that within the last couple of years Robert had beaten Victor for being overly jealous of an apparently innocent relationship with Mariequita. Mademoiselle Reisz also invites Edna to visit her in the city after they have all returned for the winter.

Commentary

Not only is Edna's emerging sense of self revealed in this chapter, but also revealed is her unwillingness to give up this self that is becoming better known to her during this summer of awakening. Her sense of self is based on the sum of her private thoughts and unspoken emotions. Such thoughts constitute a self apart from her identity as a mother, an identity based on externals: certain behaviors, attitudes, and activities constitute motherhood for Edna, rather than an innate sense of connection with or responsibility for her children. Trying to convey this idea to Madame Ratignolle, she says "I would give up the unessential . . . my money . . . my life for my children; but I wouldn't give myself." Of course, in the end she will give her life, but that is no tragedy for her because she designates it "unessential."

Literary Device

Interestingly, when relaying the discussion, Chopin shows the two women's fundamental opposition by saying that they "did not appear . . . to be talking the same language." Contrast this phrase with the novel's opening description of the parrot and mockingbird that represent Edna and Mademoiselle Reisz, both very different birds who seem nonetheless to have a language in common. Mademoiselle Reisz and Edna do share an approach to life that Edna will never share with Madame Ratignolle: Both Mademoiselle Reisz and Edna in their own ways tell the truth about others and themselves. Mademoiselle Reisz tells the truth about Madame Lebrun's relationship with her sons, revealing Victor as the favorite, and offers blunt, acerbic appraisals of everyone else. Edna's means of telling the truth is to disregard the social conventions that do not correspond with her true wants and needs, as she will do after returning to New Orleans.

Theme

The theme of children as models for or reflections of a thoughtless devotion to pleasure continues in this chapter with Edna's irritation with the children for spending too much time in the sun. She "wondered why the children persisted in playing in the sun when they might be under the trees." The obvious answer is that the children were enjoying themselves where they were, living in the pleasure of the moment rather than considering the consequences. This same desire to keep playing in the sun when sunburn will inevitably result underlies Edna's later affair with Alcée Arobin. The same irritation she feels with the children now is doubtless felt by those who are left behind when she has seemingly sacrificed herself for her romantic caprices. Married to the successful, generous Léonce, Edna was securely "under the trees," safe from the elements in her upper-class society. Nevertheless, being too long "in the sun" held a much stronger appeal for her, regardless of the consequences.

Glossary

compass   here, amount.

Chapter XVII

Summary

A few weeks after their return to New Orleans for the winter, Edna decides to be out of the house on her reception day—the one day of the week when custom demands that she stay at home to receive social callers. Léonce is incensed, insisting that her snub to the other ladies could hurt his business with their husbands. Also angry that the cook prepared a poor meal, asserting that she has grown lazy under Edna's lackadaisical employment, Léonce leaves to dine at his social club. In contrast to similar incidences in the past, Edna does not lose her appetite but finishes her dinner deliberately. Then she goes to her room, where she throws her wedding band on the floor and stamps on it and smashes a vase on the hearth.

Commentary

Léonce's materialism and devotion to convention are highlighted in this chapter. When Chopin indicates that Léonce "greatly valued his possessions, chiefly because they were his," the implication is that Edna, too, is valued for that same reason rather than for her own qualities. He warns Edna that abandoning her callers on her reception day is potentially damaging to his business and by extension, their lifestyle, explaining that "it's just such seeming trifles that we've got to take seriously; such things count." His goals are strictly financial and superficial; he wants to "keep up with the procession" that is the upper-class life. Edna's priorities are no longer compatible with Léonce's—perhaps she never shared his goals but never felt strongly enough to assert her opinions through her actions.

Character Insight

Léonce's lack of interest in or respect for Edna's point of view is depicted in this scene, as he chastises her for her behavior without inquiring its cause. He treats Edna as if she were one of his employees, like the cook or one of the clerks in his office. In a sense she is an employee: acting as hostess and nanny in exchange for room and board and the sumptuous furnishings of their house. When Edna acts on her desire to be out and about on her reception day; she behaves like a woman of some independence, not one seeking her husband/employer's approval.

Style & Language

Rather than accepting any callers that evening, she spends a gloomy time in her room looking out over the garden where "[a]ll the mystery and witchery of the night seemed to have gathered." Edna's connection to the fabled dark side of the feminine spirit is indicated here: "She was seeking herself and finding herself in just such sweet, half-darkness"—an image in marked contrast to the lack of mystery and darkness in Madame Ratignolle's character or moods. This passage instead links Edna to the non-domestic women of history, the witches, saints, and mystics who cause trouble with their independent thinking in cultures that demand passivity from women.

Note, however, that while she may fling her wedding ring to the ground, "her small boot heel did not make . . . a mark upon the little glittering circlet," which she puts back on her finger when the maid finds it on the floor. Her powers are not enough to bring about an end or real change to the society which has such exacting expectations; she can and will, however, change her own responses to those demands and change her one, small life.

Glossary

Esplanade Street a mansion-lined street in New Orleans, populated primarily by upper-class Creoles.

appointments furniture; equipment.

reception day one day each week, an upper-class woman was expected to stay home and receive visitors. The day of the week was established when a woman married, and custom demanded she entertain on that day from then on.

mulatto a person who has one black parent and one white parent.

les convenances social conventions; protocol.

futures a contract for a specific commodity bought or sold for delivery at a later date.

Chapter XVIII

Summary

The next day, feeling as if all elements of her environment have become hostile, Edna retreats into an examination of some of her old sketches. She takes a few of the better ones to show Madame Ratignolle, who encourages her plan to study drawing with a teacher named Laidpore. When Monsieur Ratignolle comes home for lunch, Edna notes the harmony of the Ratignolles' marriage. Upon leaving, however, she pities them, feeling that their abiding contentment prevents them from experiencing extremes of passion.

Commentary

Although Léonce does not exhibit any hostility toward Edna on this day, Edna feels hostility emanating from all she sees—"the children, the fruit vender, the flowers . . . were all part and parcel of an alien world which had suddenly become antagonistic" to her independent spirit. Having made the small but significant break with her old world by disregarding her reception day, all has changed for Edna. She can no longer pretend that a placid domesticity suits her.

Character Insight

Madame Ratignolle provides the image of a wife that Léonce desires Edna to maintain: She is "keenly interested in everything [her husband] said, laying down her fork the better to listen." While the Ratignolles seems to have an ideal union, and Madame Ratignolle seems to be eminently fulfilled in her role as a "mother-woman," Edna pities her "for that colorless existence which never uplifted its possessor beyond the region of blind contentment . . . in which she would never have the taste of life's delirium."

Interestingly, as she thinks this thought, Edna ponders the meaning of the phrase "life's delirium," a phrase that seems to come to her out of nowhere. Delirium is a state of extreme excitement often resulting in hallucinations that seem quite real and may be intensely joyful, as in the phrase "deliriously happy." Yet a delirium can also bring pain, as in the violent hallucinations of delirium tremens. Either way, a delirium induces experiences that are not grounded in reality. Furthering this idea is Chopin's description of Edna as "still under the spell of her infatuation" with Robert—like the Gulf spirit whom Edna supposedly captivated, Robert has captured her.

Perhaps Edna longs for delirium over her actual life because she feels she has no escape from it. In fact, her options are fairly limited, given the socio-economic restrictions on women at that time. Divorce was unthinkable. When she looks at the "domestic harmony" of the Ratignolles, she "could see in it but an appalling and hopeless ennui"—a reflection of her own experience with the enforced domesticity of her lifestyle.

Literary Device

Yet she looks to Madame Ratignolle to help her "put heart into her venture" of studying with an art instructor, knowing that Madame Ratignolle will respond enthusiastically (if not knowledgeably) and with great praise for Edna's work. Contrast Edna's desires for praise, no matter how cheaply won, with Mademoiselle Reisz's refusal to play for most of the vacationers at Grand Isle. Mademoiselle Reisz is confident of her fully developed artistry, a state Edna has not achieved.

Glossary

banquette   a raised way; sidewalk.

porte cochère   a large entrance gateway into a courtyard.

soirée musicale   a party or gathering in the evening.

Better a dinner of herbs   Refers to the biblical passage Proverbs 15:17—"Better a dinner of herbs where love is, than a fattened ox and hatred therewith."

Chapter XIX

Summary

Edna moves into full-fledged rebellion. She abandons all social and household duties, spending time instead painting in a small studio she's set up on the top floor of their house. As she paints, she mentally recalls the details of her time with Robert and sings the song "*si tu savais*" which he sang to her. Her consistent insubordination causes Léonce to wonder about her mental health.

Commentary

Edna's lack of true artistry is further depicted in this chapter. On her bad days, "when life appeared to her like a grotesque pandemonium," she is not inspired by the darkness of human experience and emotion, as the great painters are. Instead she paints when she is happy, reveling in the sensuality of existence when "her whole being seemed to be one with the sunlight, the colors, the odors" of her world.

These extremes of emotion do satisfy her newly insistent desire for a life passionately lived. In that respect, Edna has gotten what she wants.

Edna admits her lack of artistry to Léonce, agreeing with his assessment that she is not in fact a true painter. Yet Léonce's insight ends there; he feels she is possibly losing her mind when she is, in reality, finding her true self, a self that rejects the role of housewife and the pro-forma socializing that accompanies her role in society.

Glossary

en bonne ménagère   as a good housewife.

atelier   a studio or workshop, especially one used by an artist.

Chapter XX

Summary

In one of her dark moods, Edna decides to visit Mademoiselle Reisz. She cannot find her address, so in an effort to track her down, she goes to her last known address and then thinks to visit Madame Lebrun. There Edna learns that Robert has sent his mother two letters but with no message for or mention of Edna. Madame Lebrun gives Mademoiselle Reisz's address to Edna, who leaves to make that visit. Victor notes that something about Edna seems quite different, assessing it as a change for the better.

Commentary

Edna locates her friend's address only with difficulty and "her desire to see Mademoiselle Reisz had increased tenfold since these unlooked-for obstacles had arisen to thwart it." Her response to the temporary unattainability of her friend is another expression of Edna's propensity for desiring the unobtainable, the forbidden—a lifelong feature exaggerated by her newly flourishing rebellious soul. She has a contrarian's spirit, desiring that which is denied for perhaps no more reason than the denial. This aspect of her character casts doubt on the sincerity of the infatuations she has experienced throughout her life, including her current obsession with Robert.

Note that Madame Lebrun's house appears prison-like, dominated by iron bars that "were a relic of the old *régime* . . . no one had ever thought of dislodging them." The bars symbolize social constraints on women that may not be necessary or appropriate but remain in place out of custom and lack of conscious examination. Edna is looking to take the bars off her life and forge her own path.

Victor, ever the rebel, recognizes the new development in her character, remarking to his mother that the "city atmosphere has improved her. Some way she doesn't seem like the same woman." Indeed she finds herself indulging Victor in his wild, slightly off-color stories of his adventures in the city, "remembering too late that she should have been dignified and reserved." Victor is as charismatic as his brother, successful in engaging Edna's lust for life, as his appearance at Edna's party in Chapter XXX attests.

Glossary

chambres garnies   furnished rental rooms.

Régime   (1766–1803) the period of time when the Spanish ruled the territory containing New Orleans.

scintillant   that gives off sparks; that flashes or sparkles.

colored   altered, influenced, distorted, or exaggerated to some degree.

Chapter XXI

Summary

Edna visits Mademoiselle Reisz, who is delighted to see her. She tells Edna she has received a letter from Robert in which he spoke constantly of Edna and asked Mademoiselle Reisz to play Chopin's "Impromptu" for her. Edna convinces Mademoiselle Reisz to allow her to read Robert's letter. She also laughingly informs Mademoiselle Reisz that she is becoming a painter, to which Mademoiselle Reisz replies that artists require "brave souls." While Mademoiselle Reisz plays the Chopin piece, Edna reads the letter and weeps with emotion, moved by the music and the indirect contact with Robert. She leaves in tears, asking leave to come visit again.

Commentary

This chapter is significant for its presentation of Mademoiselle Reisz's abode, an apartment highly symbolic of her life and of the life of an artist and independent person. Mademoiselle Reisz tries to avoid the traffic of ordinary life, choosing a top floor apartment to "discourage the approach of beggars, peddlers, and callers." Her unrelenting honesty about human nature and the prescribed niceties of genteel culture underlie her desire to be removed from such pedestrian distractions.

Mademoiselle Reisz's frank appraisal of others' behaviors and virtues (or lack thereof) renders her unlikable to most everyone. Her respect for honesty is such, however, that she is "greatly pleased" by Edna's candid admission that she doesn't know whether or not she actually likes her.

Character Insight

Mademoiselle Reisz's isolation, both physical and social, provides more time for her art and herself. Yet there are disadvantages to her existence, as well. While she has many windows in her front room (the equivalent of a living room), they are terribly dirty, a testament to not only her lack of interest in housekeeping but also to the economic limits on single women. If she had married, she could likely afford plusher accommodations and a servant or two. The windows' filthy condition doesn't matter much, however, because they are "nearly always open," allowing in "a good deal of smoke and soot; but at the same time all the light and air that there was." With the freedom of fresh air comes the soot and smoke but Mademoiselle Reisz has learned to live with the bad that accompanies the good—just as she has learned to live with the physical and societal limitations of a single woman who insists on telling the truth.

Literary Device

The depiction of freedom's limitations continues with the description of her three small rooms: A "magnificent piano crowded the apartment" while she has only a gas stove for cooking and "a rare old buffet, dingy and battered" in which to keep her things. The contents of her apartment reflect her priorities. While her surroundings are not particularly comfortable, they are *hers*, maintained under her own terms. Mademoiselle Reisz is not attractive, rich, or well liked but has carved out an independent life nonetheless. As she plays for Edna, the music "floated out upon the night" just as the mockingbird of the first chapters, her symbolic counterpart, was "whistling his fluty notes out upon the breeze with maddening persistence." Although caged, he mocks listeners with his insistence on playing his own tune just as Mademoiselle Reisz taunts others with her honesty and independence of thought and lifestyle.

Theme

Also significant in this chapter is Mademoiselle Reisz's definition of an artist as a person who not only possesses "absolute gifts—which have not been acquired by one's own effort" but also a "brave soul. The soul that dares and defies." In this definition, the efforts of hard work and practice matter less than an innate, indisputable talent and the courage to use those talents to produce work true to itself, true to an individual vision that defies the dictates of tradition or convention.

In response to this pronouncement, Edna does not ask for clarification or offer an opinion herself; she asks only to see Robert's letter again and hear the music piece he'd mentioned. Her interests lie more with pursuing love than with developing her art. Yet in her pursuit of love, which is both incidental to and coincident with her discovery of her self, Edna shows she has the heart to dare and defy, to act in accordance with her own wishes despite extreme pressure to uphold her conventional role as faithful wife and mother. She has made passion her main priority.

From the letter Robert has written Mademoiselle Reisz, clearly he reciprocates Edna's passion for him. With the socially withdrawn Mademoiselle Reisz, he feels comfortable ostensibly revealing his obsession with Edna; she is far from being a gossip and dislikes everyone who is. Almost as if foreseeing the result of this inappropriate love, Mademoiselle Reisz intermingles her performance of the Chopin piece with the "quivering love-notes of Isolde's song," invoking the theatrical death of another woman who was in love with a man other than her husband.

Glossary

prunella a strong worsted twill, used, especially formerly, as for clerical gowns, shoe uppers, and so on.

gaiter a cloth or leather covering for the instep and ankle, and, sometimes, the calf of the leg; spat or legging.

la belle dame beautiful woman.

Isolde the Irish princess of medieval legend who was betrothed to King Mark of Cornwall and loved by Tristram, the king's nephew. The legend was made into a famous opera by Richard Wagner.

Chapter XXII

Summary

Léonce visits an old family friend, Dr. Mandelet, seeking advice about Edna. Léonce reveals that she has abandoned her domestic and social duties, become moody, and has stopped having sex with him. Further, Edna is refusing to attend her sister's wedding, asserting that a wedding is a highly regrettable occasion. The doctor concludes that another man is probably the cause, a suspicion he does not share with Léonce. Instead, he advises Léonce to leave Edna alone to work the moodiness out of her system and promises to come to dinner to unobtrusively examine her.

Commentary

Character Insight

In Chapter V, Chopin notes that "the Creole husband is never jealous; with him the gangrene passion is one which has become dwarfed by disuse." Léonce himself testifies proudly to the doctor that he is "of that old Creole race of Pontelliers that dry up and finally blow away." In his family background are no deaths due to duels or heartbreak, no fatal crimes of passion that result in a romantic end. This background information explains Léonce's lack of perception as he outlines to Dr. Mandelet the behavior of a woman clearly in love with someone other than her husband. The doctor grasps the true nature of Edna's disinterest in society and sex but does not put forth his suspicion to Léonce. One outcome of such a suggestion might be Léonce confronting Edna about her romance, a confrontation for which the passionless Léonce is ill equipped. By advising him to "let her alone," the doctor hopes that the suspected affair will subside of its own volition.

Glossary

en bon ami   as a friend.

à Jeudi   until Thursday.

Chapter XXIII

Summary

Edna's father, the Colonel, comes to visit. They spend time at the racetrack, where they socialize with Mrs. Merriman, Mrs. Highcamp, and Alcée Arobin. Dr. Mandelet comes to dinner one night and is alarmed by Edna's high-spirited recollection of their day at the races—he fears she is already enamored of Arobin, a notorious womanizer. During dinner, the doctor tells a story about a married woman who fell in love with another man but returned her devotion to her husband in the end. Edna, nonplussed, counters with a vivid tale of her own about a couple in love who rowed away one night in a small boat and disappeared in the Baratarian Islands, never to be seen again.

Commentary

This chapter reveals that Edna lacks the art of flirting. This lack of flirtatiousness is ironic, given her later affair with Arobin, which is based entirely on sexual chemistry. Disinterest in coquetry aside, her burgeoning sensuality is evident to others.

Character Insight

Dr. Mandelet notes that Edna is no longer "the listless woman he had known" but reminds him of "some beautiful, sleek animal waking up in the sun." Note that as everyone tells stories at the dinner table, each person's story indicates some measure of the teller's personality. Léonce's tale is a superficial reminiscence of a traditional childhood, while the Colonel, as the retention of his title suggests, still strongly identifies with his role in "those dark and bitter days" of the Civil War. Desiring to instruct Edna, the doctor offers a parable of a woman's love returning her husband, a lesson that is lost on Edna.

Her tale, which she makes up on the spot, is really a description of her ideal resolution to her current situation. The elements of her story are based on her one entire day spent with Robert on the *Chênière*, including the fictitious disclaimer that she'd heard the story from Madame Antoine. Note that the story lacks true resolution, offering only that "a woman . . . paddled away with her lover one night in a pirogue and never came back." For Edna, this story is not about the ending; it is all about the detail—the experience rather than consequences. While the story lacks a true ending, indicating that Edna herself does not know where her love for Robert will take her, it does not lack for sensual detail. In her telling, she is able to viscerally convey to her listeners the lovers' experience: "They could feel the hot breath of the southern night, they could hear the long sweep of the pirogue through the glistening moonlit water."

Literary Device

Edna's evident emotional involvement in the story and the coincidental meeting with Arobin that day concerns the doctor, who has a keen understanding of human behavior and knows too Arobin's reputation for seducing other men's wives. Ironically, he has cause for concern; two clues dropped previously in the text indicate that Edna has fallen in with a bad crowd. In Chapter VIII, Robert defends his platonic relationship with Edna by saying "Now if I were like Arobin— you remember Alcée Arobin . . . and that consul's wife" and in Chapter XVII Léonce tells Edna "the less you have to do with Mrs. Highcamp, the better" because her husband made for a poor business prospect.

Glossary

perambulation   a walking about; a stroll.

soirée musicale   an event or party dedicated to musical performance.

coquetry   the behavior or act of a coquette; flirting.

bourgeois   middle-class; also used variously to mean conventional, smug, materialistic, and so on.

toddy   a drink of brandy or whiskey with hot water, sugar, and often, spices.

darky   an African-American; a derogatory or contemptuous term.

grosbec   any of various passerine birds with a thick, strong, conical bill. Usually spelled grosbeak.

pirogue   a dugout canoe.

Chapter XXIV

Summary

Edna is glad when her father's visit is over, tired of arguing with him over her refusal to attend her sister's wedding. Léonce leaves as well, for an extended business trip to New York, while the boys leave for their grandmother's. Edna revels in her first taste of independent solitude, seeing the house as though for the first time.

Commentary

Theme

Edna's burst of solicitous attention toward Léonce as he leaves—"looking after his clothing, thinking about heavy underwear, quite as Madame Ratignolle would have done"—is an unconscious purging of the last vestiges of her old self. Her family's absence has granted her an incredible freedom that she has never known before and that she thoroughly relishes. Her new freedom brings new perspective and new choices. How appropriate that her reading choice that first night is the transcendental writer Ralph Waldo Emerson, who placed greater value on emotion and intuition than on reason or rationalism. That night she goes to bed with a greater sense of peace than she has ever experienced—one last great peace before her affair with Arobin begins.

Glossary

on her mettle   roused or prepared to do her best.

marron glacé   marrons in syrup or glazed with sugar; candied chestnuts.

Emerson   Ralph Waldo Emerson (1803–1882); U.S. essayist, philosopher, and poet.

eiderdown   a quilt stuffed with the soft, fine breast feathers or down of the eider duck.

Chapter XXV

Summary

Edna still cannot work on her art on gloomy days, so she spends rainy days either at home moping or seeking solace by visiting friends. She spends more time at the racetrack with Arobin and Mrs. Highcamp. Her increasingly bold, vivacious personality attracts Arobin.

One afternoon he picks her up to again attend the races but this time Mrs. Highcamp is not with him. They go the races and then to dinner at Edna's house. After dinner he shows her a dueling scar on his wrist and she impulsively grabs his hand, then withdraws in confusion and alarm, claiming to be upset by the sight of the scar. She responds with hostility when he too-warmly kisses her hand while apologizing, feeling as though she is being unfaithful to Robert (but not to Léonce).

Commentary

Character Insight

In Chapter XXIII, Edna sketches out her perfect scene of two lovers in a boat disappearing in the night—a scene without end or resolution. This chapter reveals Edna has the same focus on process over goal with regard to her art: "being devoid of ambition, and striving not toward accomplishment, she drew satisfaction from the work in itself." Her inability to work when the weather is less than sunny prevents her from becoming a great artist. She is far more interested in doing what feels good rather than producing something of worth, an attitude that dominates her life and underlies her imminent affair with Arobin.

Edna is primed for a meaningless tryst after her success at the racetrack. Intoxicated by the excitement and adrenaline, she "wanted something to happen—something, anything, she did not know what." She is not explicitly interested in having an affair with anyone other than Robert; Arobin is simply in the right place at the right time.

Literary Device

While she has no romantic feelings for Arobin, when he shows her the scar on his wrist she experiences a strong, "spasmodic" impulse compelling "her fingers to close in a sort of clutch upon his hand." Such a description of her movement, so mechanical and purely physical, is indicative of Arobin's physical appeal to Edna, although he holds no emotional appeal for her.

Arobin's seduction of married women invites them to a sort of rebellion—making Edna a prime target at this point in her life. She finds that "the effrontery in his eyes repelled the old, vanishing self in her, yet drew all her awakening sensuousness." That sensuousness is greatly appealing to Arobin, and he has the experience to exploit it for his own ends. When she is with Arobin, Edna is under the influence of another intoxicant; although he has no emotional or romantic hold on her, "his lips upon her hand had acted like a narcotic upon her."

Although intrigued at some level by Arobin's overtures, she can't help but feel as though she is being unfaithful to Robert, who currently has her heart, although Léonce's feelings, who has her hand in marriage, are not a concern. The evening's physical stimulation, a sensual awakening, is followed by "a languorous sleep" in which the narcotic of excitement provided by the gambling at the track and the dicey involvement with Arobin causes "vanishing dreams"—as if Edna's innocence about her own sexual desires is also vanishing.

Glossary

drag   a type of private stagecoach of the nineteenth century, with seats inside and on top, drawn by four horses.

Jockey Club   a luxurious social club limited to a select group of the New Orleans upper class.

gelding   a gelded animal; especially, a castrated male horse.

Dante   Dante Alighieri (1265–1321); Italian poet: wrote *The Divine Comedy*.

Grieg   Edvard Grieg (1843–1907); Norwegian composer.

car   here, streetcar.

cicatrice   car.

Chapter XXVI

Summary

Arobin embarrasses Edna with an emotional letter of apology for upsetting her the night before, and this irritates her: The next day she feels as though she'd taken the kiss on her hand too seriously. She writes a deliberately light and playful note in response. After that, they see each nearly every day.

Edna visits Mademoiselle Reisz, whose music always soothes her. She reveals her plan to move out of Léonce's house and into a tiny rental house nearby, which she can afford due to her racetrack winnings and sales of her drawings, and her desire to give an elaborate dinner party before moving from her old house. Reading Robert's latest letter, Edna is ecstatic to learn that he is returning soon. In response to Mademoiselle Reisz's questioning, Edna reveals that she loves Robert simply because she does, and that when he is back she will do nothing more than be happy.

Ironically, she is so happy at the news of his return that she sends a box of bonbons to her children and writes a cheerful, spirited note to Léonce in which she tells him of her plans to move out.

Commentary

Interesting similarities between Edna's summertime relationship with Robert and her current relationship with Arobin are revealed in this chapter. Just as she had grown used to Robert's presence, missing him when he was gone although she took him for granted when he was near, now Edna "grew accustomed to" Arobin's presence. And just as her then-dominant prudery caused her to blush when Robert told slightly racy anecdotes or made open references to other women's pregnancies, Arobin "sometimes talked in a way that . . . brought the crimson into her face; in a way that pleased her at last, appealing to the animalism that stirred impatiently within her."

Yet Arobin has not replaced Robert in her heart. The news that he is returning to New Orleans fills her with joy. Note that once again Mademoiselle Reisz uses her music to set the mood for Edna's reading of the letter, just as she did on Edna's first visit (in Chapter XXI) when she worked Isolde's tragic song into the Chopin "Impromptu." Now, knowing the letter's contents, she plays a warm, bright piece that she "prepared [Edna] for joy and exultation."

Edna's plans for his return are unrealistic, however. When Mademoiselle Reisz asks what she will do upon his return, Edna replies "Do? Nothing, except feel glad and happy to be alive." Her passionate feelings are not of the nature that will let her simply rejoice at his return without eventually seeking him out, and seeking verification of Mademoiselle Reisz's appraisal that "he loves you, poor fool, and is trying to forget you." Edna is already subconsciously preparing for his return by taking her own house, where she can conduct herself as she pleases and with whom she pleases, and wherein everything is provided by herself rather than by her husband's income and goodwill. She does not seem to be conscious of the fact that she is leaving her husband, thinking only that when Léonce returned there "would have to be an understanding, an explanation. Conditions would some way adjust themselves."

Mentally she has already moved out, using the past tense when she tells Mademoiselle Reisz that Léonce's house "never seemed like mine, anyway." Her spirit is growing stronger, enabling her to take this drastic step and improve her artwork, as well. Her new development is evident in her work, which is good enough to provide a small income as, according to her art teacher and broker Laidpore, it "grows in force and individuality." When Mademoiselle Reisz tells Edna that if she herself were still young she'd fall in love with an ambitious, talented man, not "a man of ordinary caliber," she hints that Robert may not be able to keep up with Edna as her whole being continues to grow with "force and individuality."

Glossary

grand esprit   great spirit.

ma reine   my queen (or my love).

Chapters **XXVII** and **XXVIII**

Summary

Arobin visits Edna that night. She is still exhilarated at the thought of Robert's imminent return but does not reveal the reason for her good mood to Arobin. She does tell him about Mademoiselle Reisz's unusual gesture of feeling Edna's shoulder blades "to see if my wings were strong," and her explanation that Edna must have strong wings to fly beyond society's expectations. As she relates this anecdote to Arobin, he is stroking her hair and face. Then he leans his face forward to kiss her and she responds immediately with ardor, pulling him toward her. It is the most physically charged kiss of her life.

Chapter XXVIII reveals that after Arobin leaves, Edna feels a storm of emotions, even crying briefly, but overall feels no shame. Having experienced the thrill of an intensely sexual kiss for the first time, she regrets only that it was not with Robert.

Commentary

Significantly, Edna does not tell Arobin the true reason for her high spirits. Not only does she see a great need for secrecy about her feelings for Robert but knowledge of them may ruin the atmosphere of sexual tension that is firmly in place around herself and Arobin. She loves Robert but she enjoys Arobin's skilled attention and seductive manner, "the touch of his fingers through her hair." The chemistry between them is such that even her lack of emotional connection with him doesn't detract from the intensity of the kiss, "the first kiss of her life to which her nature had really responded. It was a flaming torch that kindled desire."

Now she knows the experience of a passionate sexual connection, which has been missing so far in her life. Even before the kiss occurs, she refers to herself as "a devilishly wicked specimen" of womankind, according to conventional morality, for loving Robert and endeavoring to move out of her husband's house. "But some way I can't convince myself that I am"—she is instinctively judging herself by another code of ethics, one in which being true to herself takes priority over commitments erroneously made in the ignorance of youth.

To adhere to this alternate set of morals requires personal strength, however, as Mademoiselle Reisz is fully aware of. She tests Edna metaphorically, physically feeling for her symbolic wings, and warns her explicitly about the fate of those who seek to "soar above the level plain of tradition and prejudice" but who lack the fortitude to maintain flight and end up "bruised, exhausted, fluttering back to earth." Mademoiselle Reisz's warning serves as a grim foreshadowing of Edna's final scene, when she reaches the beach on Grand Isle and sees a bird with a broken wing sinking ominously through the air to the water.

Yet this evening Edna is far from sinking, exhausted, to earth. She does feel the reproach of the other men in her life both internally, as her love for Robert protectively increases in response to Arobin's kiss, and externally, surrounded as she is by Léonce's household goods. Overall, however, she is gratified by the discovery of a red-hot kiss, a kiss that exemplifies the passion of lovers throughout history, which she herself has never experienced first hand.

Her passionate attachments had always been to men unavailable for a stolen kiss; her attraction to Léonce, as related in Chapter VII, was based more on "his absolute devotion" to her, which she found quite flattering but did not inflame her with love or lust. Only now, with Arobin's kiss, does she get to know the results of potent sexual chemistry, again "appealing to the animalism that stirred impatiently within her" (Chapter XXVI).

Yet because the appeal of the experience was purely sensual, she regrets that it was not further augmented by an emotional connection, that it was lust and "not love which had held this cup of life to her lips."

Glossary

tabouret   a low, upholstered footstool. Also spelled taboret.

multitudinous   very numerous; many.

Chapter XXIX

Summary

The day after the kiss, Edna hurries to gather her things to move out of the house she shares with Léonce into the "pigeon house" she has rented, so called because of its small size. Arobin arrives and helps with the preparations, then Edna sends him away, insisting that he wait to see her until the next day's dinner party.

Commentary

Style & Language

After Edna has kissed Arobin, she feels a greater impetus to remove herself from the surroundings provided and dominated by Léonce. She feverishly packs, like "one who has entered . . . some forbidden temple in which a thousand muffled voices bade her begone." The reference to a temple invokes the image of a church, and recalls the morning after her desire first stirred for Robert, when she could not sit through the church service but had to flee the church's oppressive air. Further, by ostensibly leaving Léonce, she is disregarding her marriage vows, not a course of action taken lightly by the Catholic church under whose auspices she was married. Those "thousand muffled voices" she hears are the voices of disapproval raised in her culture when a woman declares her independence or desire for freedom.

Yet Edna is in earnest about her bid for freedom, taking from the house only those things she had acquired herself. She is at her apex of caprice and self-indulgence, taking "no moment of deliberation between the thought and its fulfillment," a non-contemplative state that allows no moment to consider the consequences of her move or of last night's kiss.

Although she is reluctant to look Arobin in the eye and avoids being alone in a room with him, she clearly does not regret the physical contact with him. Insisting that he wait until tomorrow's dinner party to see her again, she "looked at him with eyes that at once gave him courage to wait and made it torture to wait." Her sexual awakening is accelerated along with her move.

Significantly, however, she is still in effect a caged bird (recall the parrot symbolism of Chapter I). While escaping the gilded cage that is Léonce's house, she is moving into a pigeon house, which is a small bird-house meant for keeping domesticated pigeons. Although the pigeon house will allow her more latitude to come and go as she pleases, still she is domesticated, limited by other restraints such as those society places on women and Robert's concession to those expectations.

Glossary

pigeon house small bird house for domesticated pigeons.

coup d'état the sudden, forcible overthrow of a ruler or government, sometimes with violence, by a small group of people already having some political or military authority.

cravat a necktie.

plumb perfectly vertical; straight down.

Chapters XXX and XXXI

Summary

Ten guests show up for Edna's dinner party: Arobin, Mademoiselle Reisz, Victor Lebrun, Mrs. Highcamp, Monsieur Ratignolle, and a few others. Edna announces that it is her twenty-ninth birthday. Despite the party's success, she longs for Robert. When Victor later begins to drunkenly sing the song Robert sang to Edna, "Si tu savais," she is so upset she accidentally breaks her wineglass and then puts her hand over Victor's mouth to make him stop singing. The party breaks up soon after.

Chapter XXXI begins with Arobin helping Edna lock up the mansion and walking her to the pigeon house. She is overwrought and miserable, missing Robert and feeling hopeless. Once inside, Arobin presses his advantage, and they become lovers that night.

Commentary

The depiction of Edna at her party as "the regal woman, the one who rules, who looks on, who stands alone" grants her simultaneously command and loneliness, just as one frequently accompanies the other in life. Contrast this queenly image with Chapter V's description of Madame Ratignolle as having "the grace and majesty which queens . . . possess." Her power is based on nurturing others; Edna's power comes from dedication to pleasing herself. As a woman who is taking charge of her life's direction and steering it in an unpopular direction, she is isolating herself from mainstream society—and from those individuals who cannot admit they would like to make the same move.

Yet for all her strength, all the progress she has made in discovering her true self, she is nonetheless unhappy without Robert at her side. Chopin uses significant word choices in describing Edna's longing, however: "she felt the old ennui . . . the hopelessness which . . . came upon her like an obsession." Is her obsession with Robert himself or with the high drama and emotional intrigue that accompanies her inappropriate love for him?

Literary Device

One of her guests, Gouvernail, makes a reference to desire as "a graven image," as a thing in itself to be worshipped, when he quotes the first two lines from Swinburne's "The Cameo" in response to Victor's splendid appearance at the dinner table. With their combined histories of courting the unattainable, Edna and Robert have spent years desiring for the sake of desiring, erecting emotional facades. Their current obsession with each other, more substantial than any other previously experienced, is more dangerous for the physical passion Edna brings to it. The ominous Swinburne line "Painted with red blood on a ground of gold" casts the entire venture of love as bound for failure and catastrophe, although it may be a grand, golden disaster.

Desire is an ancient and sometimes brutal urge, as indicated in Swinburne's phrase "graven image," which evokes images of harsh primal gods. The strength of desire is evident when Edna feels Victor's kiss on her palm as a "pleasing sting"—she is not immune to the charms of her beloved's brother, as harsh a truth as that may be. Victor appeals to her great sensuality just as Arobin does. At this dinner he plays the role of the extreme sensualist, drawing out the same quality in Edna; recall her playful response to his racy stories in Chapter XX, to which she meant to respond with disapproval.

Character Insight

Mademoiselle Reisz plays a role that is a counterpart to Doctor Mandelet's. While at the dinner with Léonce, the Colonel and Edna, the doctor sought to instruct Edna with his parable of a married woman's wandering heart; he could discern in her behavior the telltale signs. Mademoiselle Reisz, too, knows human nature well and probably intuits the brewing affair between Edna and Arobin. As she leaves the party, she warns Edna to "behave well." Her advice is not heeded, however, as Edna's disheartenment over Robert's absence from her life makes her vulnerable to Arobin's now-serious advances.

Always a persuasive charmer, Arobin accelerates his wooing of Edna by having her little house filled with flowers while they are at the dinner. On this night, crushed by Victor's rendition of the song Robert sang to her once, the song that underscores his unattainability then and his absence now, Edna is in need of an understanding friend. With Arobin stroking her hair, Edna feels comforted and "could have fallen quietly asleep there if he had continued to pass his hand over her hair." Yet he is not content to provide only solace but presses his advantage until "she had become supple to his gentle, seductive entreaties." She loves Robert but he has left her for Mexico and here is Arobin with his incessant charm and gentle caress. No wonder Edna is greatly conflicted at this moment, her voice "uneven" as she asks whether he is leaving. In her first night at the pigeon house, she consummates her flirtation with Arobin.

Glossary

souffrante   suffering or ill; here, a reference to the late stage of pregnancy.

shallow-pate   a person lacking depth or intelligence.

alacrity   eager willingness or readiness, often manifested by quick, lively action.

lorgnette   a pair of eyeglasses attached to a handle.

nom de guerre   a pseudonym.

mets   main dish or main course.

entre-mets   a dish served between the main courses or as a side dish.

pompano   any of various edible, marine North American and West Indian jack fishes.

jessamine   any of various tropical and subtropical plants of the olive family, with fragrant flowers of yellow, red, or white, used in perfumes or for scenting tea. Typically spelled jasmine.

Bonne nuit, ma reine, soyez sage   Good night, my queen, behave well.

Ce que tes yeux me disent   What your eyes are saying to me.

parterre   an ornamental garden area in which the flower beds and path form a pattern.

matting   a woven fabric of fiber, as straw or hemp, for mats, floor covering, wrapping, and so on.

Chapter XXXII

Summary

When Léonce receives Edna's letter telling him of her plans to move into her own little house, he is concerned about how this move might look to his current and prospective clients. Feeling that they'll think he can't afford the large house, he contracts long-distance with architects and workers to renovate his mansion, and places a notice in the paper announcing the renovations and also the Pontelliers' intention to spend the summer abroad while work is completed. He never considers that Edna might have left him, not merely the house. Meanwhile, Edna makes the little pigeon house her own home.

She then spends a week with her children and mother-in-law in the country. Edna relishes her time with the boys and leaves them with a great regret, which disappears by the time she reaches New Orleans where she feels once again freed by the solitude and simplicity of her new life.

Commentary

Character Insight

How ironic that this chapter opens with Léonce's strong objections to Edna's moving when the previous chapter provided far more serious grounds for his displeasure. Léonce, true to his character, places prime importance on their reputations, seeking to shield his reputation in the business world. He is not concerned with Edna's feelings, the emotional causes of her move, but implores her "to consider first, foremost, and above all else, what people would say." Handicapped by a lack of jealousy or understanding of passion, he never considers that his wife might have undertaken the move to free herself of him. Instead he acts quickly and decisively to stage an alibi for Edna's inexplicable action, arranging long-distance a renovation of the house. Chopin employs a rarely used and well-placed exclamation point to convey his relief at effectively remedying the situation (and to indicate his main priority): "Mr. Pontellier had saved appearances!"

Contrasting sharply with Léonce's frenetic materialism is Edna's quiet, decisive growth towards realizing her true self. "There was with her a feeling of having descended in the social scale, with a corresponding . . . [ascent] in the spiritual." In her small house filled with a few simple items, having shed not only the large house but the public-relations lifestyle that came with it, she is freed to "look with her own eyes . . . to apprehend the deeper currents of life."

Significantly, she chooses this point in time to spend a week with her children at their grandmother's. She had told Madame Ratignolle in Chapter XVI that "I would give my life for my children; but I wouldn't give myself." During this visit, however, "giving them all of herself, and . . . filling herself with their young existence," she does give her self but takes emotional sustenance and vitality from them in return. This exchange marks a return to the theme of sensuality as the realm of childhood. Edna's approach to her marital situation seems somewhat childish: When the boys ask where they and Léonce will sleep in her new house, she tells that "the fairies would fix it all right." In fact she has no recourse other than fairies to resolve the situation to everyone's satisfaction. "Conditions would some way adjust themselves, she felt," when in Chapter XXVI she considered what would happen when Léonce returned. Like her story about the two lovers disappearing in the night, her attitude toward Léonce's return indicates that Edna is more focused on the experience rather than consequences.

Literary Device

During her stay with the boys, Edna is overjoyed to see them, leaving them "with a wrench and a pang," carrying the experience of them with her like a song in her head—a song that disappears from her mind by the time she reaches her new home. In contrast, the song that Robert sang to her, "Si tu savais," haunts her still, an indication of her deeper allegiance to him and all he represents.

Glossary

ménage   a household; domestic establishment.

snuggery   a snug or comfortable place, room, and so on.

frescoing   painting with watercolors on wet plaster.

Chapters XXXIII, XXXIV, and XXXV

Summary

Madame Ratignolle visits Edna in the pigeon house and warns her of gossip concerning her relationship with Arobin. Later that day, Edna is waiting in Mademoiselle Reisz's apartment for Reisz to return when Robert appears. Both are shocked to see each other, and Edna is hurt that he has been back in New Orleans for two days and has not sought her out. Robert walks Edna home, and is shocked to find a photograph of Arobin among her sketches. She explains that she had been using the photo to sketch Arobin's portrait.

After telling her his thoughts and feelings while in Mexico, he feels she is mocking him and pronounces her cruel. They sit in silence until dinner is ready.

In Chapter XXXIV, Edna and Robert eat a simple dinner, keeping the conversation away from the emotional underpinnings of their relationship. Edna is jealous when she discovers that his tobacco pouch was a gift from a young woman in Vera Cruz. Arobin arrives and by chance comments on the remarkable beauty of Vera Cruz women. Robert leaves and Arobin lingers to read the paper and smoke a cigar. Edna sends him away and reviews the last few hours with Robert, disappointed overall.

Chapter XXXV shows Edna the next morning full of hope, feeling that she and Robert can overcome any obstacles to their love. When Robert does not visit her that day, however, she despairs, a pattern that repeats itself for days as he continues to stay away from her. Yet she avoids places where she might see him, to avoid disappointment. Her affair with Arobin continues.

Commentary

Theme

Madame Ratignolle continues the depiction of Edna as childish, telling her that "you seem to me like a child, Edna. You seem to act without a certain amount of reflection which is necessary in this life." Madame Ratignolle speaks of the circumspection adults are expected to engage in, such as the care Léonce wishes Edna to act with. Edna's entire personality has assumed the willfulness of a child since her return from Grand Isle: She wants it all 'her way' much like a toddler.

Madame Ratignolle also raises the issue of Edna's endangered reputation, saying "you know how evil-minded the world is—someone was talking of Alcée Arobin visiting you." Just as the Pontellier mansion in the midst of renovations "looked broken and half torn asunder," so, too, does the Pontellier marriage appear—a juicy subject for the high-society women whose company Edna has shunned. Note here that when Edna is told of Arobin's lethal reputation, she remains indifferent: She has no emotional investment in Arobin or in society's good opinion.

Literary Device

She has invested time and energy into imagining her first meeting with Robert and is unprepared for the harsh reality of their first encounter. Their route to Edna's house takes them through a decidedly non-romantic, even sordid neighborhood, "picking their way across muddy streets and sidewalks encumbered with the cheap display of small tradesmen." Rarely in the novel does Chopin describe a physically unpleasant scene; she uses the device here to underscore Edna's disillusionment with the reality of seeing Robert.

When they reach her home, Robert finds a photograph of Arobin. His reaction confirms the low opinion other men have of Arobin: "do you think his head is worth drawing?" Naturally Edna does not reveal the nature of her relationship with Arobin, but presses Robert to tell her what he thought about while in Mexico. His answer, that he thought of nothing but his summer on Grande Isle and felt like a "lost soul," holds some indication for her that she was on his mind. When she responds to his question about her thoughts with a near verbatim rendition of his answer, he says she is cruel, as if she is taunting him for dwelling on their time together rather than signaling that her thoughts were with him, as well.

Style & Language

The most interesting aspect of Chapter XXXIV is the depiction of the familiarity that Arobin's and Edna's relationship has assumed. While she writes a note to their mutual friend—whom both are tired of—he has a cigar and makes himself comfortable with the paper. She asks him the date and gives him the task of mailing the note. Then he "read to her little bits out of the newspaper, while she straightened things on the table." These activities seem less like those of clandestine lovers and more like those of a married couple. Chopin paints a homey scene, illustrating how quickly a couple can achieve an air of working familiarity, which is also a testament to how quickly passion can be replaced by familiarity.

As Edna considers (in Chapter XXXV) the reasons why Robert did not seek her out to declare his love, she decides that all the elements that constrain him—his religion, the disapproval of his family and friends, his perfunctory consideration for Léonce—"were not insurmountable; they would not hold if he really loved her." Yet Robert may find those constraints much more daunting than does Edna, as Mademoiselle Reisz implies in Chapter XXVI.

Character Insight

Continuing the affair with Arobin puts an end to the hope/despair cycle. Her involvement with the utterly self-absorbed sensualist helps her along the path of true indifference; her participation in a relationship based on nothing but sexual chemistry shows her firsthand the workings of indifference.

Glossary

party call   Women were expected to visit a party's hostess within a week of the party to thank her, if they have not attended one of her parties before.

vingt-et-un   a card game called "twenty one."

personalities   here, personal matters.

tignon   a Creole word for bun: the hair is wrapped in a scarf and the scarf is wrapped around the head.

patois   a form of a language differing generally from the accepted standard, as a provincial or local dialect.

recapitulate   to repeat briefly, as in an outline; summarize.

Chapter XXXVI

Summary

Edna again encounters Robert accidentally, this time in a deserted garden café. When she asks him why he hasn't come to see her, he responds emotionally, again calling her cruel for forcing him into disclosure of his feelings. She withdraws from emotional topics and they chat a while in the café before he sees her home. Once inside the house, without warning she kisses him and he responds by holding her close and admitting his love. Edna tells him that she is her own woman, not a possession of Léonce's to be released, but is called away to Madame Ratignolle's before she can explain herself. Robert begs hers to stay with him, but Madame Ratignolle is in labor and Edna had promised to attend the birth. Before she leaves, she makes Robert promise to remain there and wait for her to return home.

Commentary

Character Insight

Because Edna has "abandoned herself to Fate" (as noted in the Chapter XXXV), she is not surprised when Robert appears in the garden café, despite its out-of-the-way location. This indifference to circumstances recalls Mademoiselle Reisz's reaction in Chapter XXVI to Edna's news that she was moving into her own house: "Nothing ever seemed to astonish her very much." Mademoiselle Reisz has perhaps imparted to Edna some of her knowledge of human nature and the workings of the world. As Edna has become more independent, taking streetcars and walking alone through the city, she has learned that "we women learn so little of life on the whole." By striking out on her own, she has learned much about not only that is new to her, but also how much she never knew—about herself, men like Arobin, and women like Mademoiselle Reisz.

Literary Device

Another parallel between characters in this scene is in Robert's angry accusation that in her pointed questions she is, on an emotional level, asking him to "bare a wound for the pleasure of looking at it, without the intention or power of healing it." This reference recalls the physical scar that Arobin showed Edna, and emphasizes the emotionality of

Edna's relationship with Robert as opposed to the physicality of her relationship with Arobin.

Edna has gleaned much from Arobin about initiating and pursuing a physical relationship. In stark contrast with the prudery of her personality at the beginning of the novel, Edna boldly and without warning kisses Robert with a "voluptuous sting," indicating that she has learned to express herself sexually.

Theme

Overall she has learned some valuable life lessons from both Mademoiselle Reisz and Arobin—both of whom are frowned upon by the polite society she left behind: Mademoiselle Reisz for her harsh if honest opinions of others; Arobin for not respecting sexual boundaries.

Yet she gives all the credit to Robert: "It was you who awoke me last summer out of a lifelong, stupid dream," she tells him. While he may have played a part in her awakening sensuality and the accompanying sense of self discover, she has grown beyond him. She clearly is somewhat amused by the way he phrases his revelation of love, repeating back to him "Yes, we have heard of such things" when he tells her of his desperate fantasies of running away with her, another man's wife. She has her own revelation—that she is no longer Léonce's to give. In response, Robert's "face grew a little white. 'What do you mean?' he asked." While his physical reaction may spring from excitement about the possibilities, given his pattern of not following through, more likely he is frightened that at last someone is calling his bluff and inviting him to commit to daring adventure. His is not a brave, defiant soul as Edna's is. Her declaration that "we shall love each other . . . Nothing else in the world is of any consequence," is still ringing in his ears as she leaves for Madame Ratignolle's. He is enthralled by her newly acquired power of seduction for the moment—but he is gone when she returns, unable yet again to follow through.

Glossary

mulatresse   female mulatto.

Chapter XXXVII

Summary

When Edna reaches Madame Ratignolle's, she finds her friend exhausted and overwrought in her labor pains. Dr. Mandelet and a midwife also attend the birth. Edna regrets attending; the birth is a harrowing scene. Edna's own childbirth experiences do not provide useful perspective, because she was drugged with chloroform for the pain. After the birth is over and she prepares to leave, Madame Ratignolle whispers dramatically to her "Think of the children, Edna . . . Remember them!"

Commentary

Madame Ratignolle plays a provocative role in this chapter. She asked for Edna's company during her labor and delivery only as source a solace to herself. However, the incredible pain and drama of childbirth serves as a lesson to Edna, showing her what she herself actually went through—and accomplished—during her own birth experiences, which were fogged by the use of chloroform as an anesthetic. Recalling her reaction to her own deliveries, she remembers being nonplussed by the boys' presence. She saw them only as an addition to "the great unnumbered multitude of souls that come and go"—there is nothing special or endearing to her about her babies, indicating that she is not maternal by nature.

Madame Ratignolle's parting words to Edna remind Edna not only that she went through the same ordeal herself while bringing Raoul and Etienne into the world but also that by virtue of being their mother, she is still responsible for their well-being. To this point, Edna had not considered the effects of her actions on her children, how leaving their father for another man might negatively affect their lives. She has been utterly focused on experience over consequence. The boys' temporary absence has granted Edna the latitude that comes with their being out of sight and out of mind. Madame Ratignolle's insistent words, delivered with such impact in her hour of trial and accomplishment, compel Edna to rethink her devotion to fulfilling all her whims at the expense of others.

Chopin uses a provocative image in connection with Madame Ratignolle, as well: As she sits in the salon, her hair "lay in a long braid on the sofa pillow, coiled like a golden serpent." Not only is the image a reference to the serpent in the Garden of Eden, whose words to Eve caused her and all subsequent women to endure great suffering in childbirth, but it also foreshadows Edna's death. In the final chapter, the waves "coiled like serpents" around Edna's legs as she prepares for her fatal swim. The serpent braid represents knowledge and the loss of innocence—Madame Ratignolle forces Edna to witness the great suffering of childbirth and reckon with the fate of her own children, who will be subjected to the same stigma that will mark Edna if she follows her current course of action. Additionally, her children have a specific need for her in their lives, as illustrated in Chapter XIV, when Etienne was not soothed by Madame Ratignolle, but needed his mother's presence before he could go to sleep. While Edna may not be the model mother in her husband's or society's opinion, her children have an attachment to her.

Glossary

Griffe   person with one mulatto parent and one black parent.

coupé   a closed carriage seating two passengers, with a seat outside for the driver.

Chapter XXXVIII

Summary

Dr. Mandelet walks Edna home. She muses on the significance of Madame Ratignolle's parting words and on her own recent disillusionment with her life. The doctor strongly urges her to talk with him about what she is going through, offering compassionate understanding. She turns down his offer. Arriving home, she sits on the porch to regain her composure before going inside, deciding to be with Robert tonight and consider the consequences for the children tomorrow. Once inside, instead of Robert, she finds a goodbye note. She spends a sleepless night on the sofa.

Commentary

Given the events of this chapter, Edna's fatal depression seems inevitable. Doctor Mandelet succinctly expresses the crux of Edna's dissatisfaction with life as a wife and mother, asserting that "youth is given up to illusions" about the nature of marriage and motherhood. The conservative culture she was raised in promoted the idea that marriage and motherhood provided an eminently satisfying vocation for all women, regardless of their temperament or true interests. Edna believed in this illusion and so committed herself to both endeavors, only to realize that she is suited for neither, being too independent and capricious.

Mandelet implies that the concept of motherhood as an integral and inevitable part of women's lives is constructed in part by society and in part by the most basic hormonal working of human biology—society's romanticized image of motherhood "seems to be a provision of Nature; a decoy to secure mothers for the race." This illusion disregards the trauma of childbirth and the dissatisfaction that some women feel with the constraints of motherhood. If a woman in Edna's culture responds to this dissatisfaction and seeks to give up marriage and motherhood in order to follow what she feels is her true path, she is condemned outright. If Edna divorces Léonce, she will be utterly ostracized.

Literary Device

In his counsel to Edna, the doctor insists that he would understand what she is going through, should she choose to confide in him. He is well versed in human nature, after all. The discrepancy in their levels of understanding and experience is emphasized when he twice addresses her as "my child." She is a child in terms of her newly developed comprehension of life, having just awoken to the reality of her unsatisfying marriage and overall lack of interest in the lifestyle Léonce demands. In waking to her true self, she is birthing herself. And like a child, she insists "I don't want anything but my own way," an internal demand she's been fully catering to since Léonce left for New York and the children left for their grandmother's. Now she is forced to consider, like an adult, whether she owes her children enough consideration to go on living with their father and subverting her desire for independence. She has to ask herself whether she should "trample upon the little lives," leaving children who need her on a personal level and who would face on a social level the stigma of their mother's abandonment.

On this night, however, she decides to focus only on Robert, determined to consider the consequences tomorrow—"that determination had driven into her soul like a death wound," a phrase that foreshadows her suicide. Sitting on her front porch, unaware that Robert is gone, she feels "the intoxication of expectancy," recalling the intoxication of betting at the track in Chapter XXV. Her relationship with Robert is another gamble, a bet that she loses. His note indicates that he has left because of their mutual passion: "Good-by—because I love you." He is not willing to face the personal and social consequences of their relationship and probably feels he is sparing her, as well, from the storm of condemnation that will attend their affair should they pursue it. He does not understand that she is indifferent to such developments. She realizes he does not understand her in her new expression of self, and this realization plays a part in her decision to commit suicide, as evidenced in her musings in the final chapter.

Glossary

arbitrary   not fixed by rules, but left to one's judgment or choice; discretionary.

Chapter XXXIX

Summary

The scene shifts to Grand Isle, where Victor is making a few repairs during the off-season on the *pension* while flirting with Mariequita. Edna appears suddenly, saying she had come to rest for a while. Startled, Victor scurries to manage room and board for her; she requests fish for dinner and asks for towels, announcing that she is going swimming.

In reality, she plans to drown herself, having decided during her sleepless night that suicide was the only means to elude the responsibilities and obligations motherhood placed on her. She also realized that someday her passion for Robert would fade, and so had become utterly despondent.

Once on the beach, she sees a bird with a broken wing falling to its own ultimate death in the water. She puts on her bathing suit but then casts it off, standing naked on the beach and feeling as if she is seeing everything for the first time. Entering the water, she swims farther and farther out while mentally sorting through her circumstances. Her last thought is a vivid recollection of a childhood scene.

Commentary

This final chapter ends Edna's story with references to the two main themes: Edna as a child and as a bird. Recall Mademoiselle Reisz's pronouncement in Chapter XXVII that the "bird that would soar above the level plain of tradition and prejudice must have strong wings. It is a sad spectacle to see the weaklings bruised, exhausted, fluttering back to earth." Although Edna had made great progress in learning to rise above the constraints of tradition, she was brought crashing to earth by the consideration of her flight's effect on her children—a traditional obligation she is emotionally unable to disregard. By fleeing to her death, she is escaping the children who "sought to drag her into the soul's slavery for the rest of her days. But she knew a way to elude them." She has decided that losing their mother to an early death is for them preferable to losing their mother to scandal—a concession to society's prejudices. In this concession, her hard-won indifference to society's demands is defeated, likening her to the bird she sees on the beach, "reeling, fluttering, circling disabled down, down to the water." To ensure that her death is not perceived as a suicide but merely a swimming accident, she makes specific requests to Victor as to what she'd like for lunch, to emphasize her false intention to return from her swim. Thus she spares her family the scandal that would accompany a suicide, another concession to cultural prejudice.

Yet she is, in a sense, not utterly defeated. She had renewed her life by giving rein to her childlike desires to always have her way despite the wants and needs of others. Now she regresses even further, feeling "like some new-born creature, opening its eyes" while standing naked on the beach—naked as newborns arrive. Further, her final thoughts are those of her early childhood. Again, she remembers the seemingly never-ending meadows of which the sea reminds her, recalling her revelation to Madame Ratignolle in Chapter VII that "sometimes I feel this summer as if I were walking through the green meadow again; idly, aimlessly, unthinking and unguided." That description also fits her behavior since she returned to New Orleans and began to rebel against her marriage and motherhood, growing into an understanding of her true self.

In the midst of this return to childhood on the beach is her mature understanding of the nature of her feelings for Robert: "she even realized that the day would come when he, too, and the thought of him would melt out of her existence, leaving her alone." Just as Robert replaced the last of her former infatuations, he, too, would come to be replaced by someone, made unattractive to her by his accessibility. For her, the joy of such romantic obsessions lies in feeling them rather than consummating them. How appropriate, then, that her last thoughts return to the subject of her first infatuation, the cavalry officer; she hears how his "spurs . . . clanged as he walked across the porch."

Given Edna's love of sensuality, her choice of the blue Gulf waters as her final resting place, the scene of her final stand, is appropriate. Chopin emphasizes not only how the water's "touch . . . is sensuous, enfolding the body in its soft, close embrace" but also its permanence: Her use of the present tense contrasts sharply with the rest of the novel, which is all in past tense. In the sea, Edna finds an everlasting love, one who will not "melt out of her existence" like Robert and the cavalry officer.

By drowning herself, Edna is taking command of her situation as best she can, sparing Raoul and Etienne the trauma of her socially unacceptable behavior, sacrificing "the inessential" (her life) because she would never "sacrifice herself for her children," as indicated in Chapter XVI. If she were to resume her married life with Léonce, she would be sacrificing the self that she has worked so hard to birth.

Style & Language

The novel's ending is provocative because Chopin does not indicate outright that Edna dies. Her story concludes not with images of death but with a soothing yet vivid description of a childhood scene. This ambiguity recalls Edna's tale in Chapter XXIII about the young lovers who disappeared one night while boating. Edna never specified their fate, whether they had escaped to start a new life together or had met with an untimely drowning. Chopin makes use of the same ambiguity; Edna's own story ends with the reader unsure as to whether she is victorious (for coming to know her true self, achieving a brief but significant measure of independence and eluding those who would hold her back) or defeated (by the need to preserve appearances for her sons' sakes).

Glossary

scantling   a small beam or timber, especially one of small cross section, as a two-by-four.

Lucullean   as in the banquets of Lucius Lucinius Lucullus (circa 110–57 B.C.); Roman general and consul: proverbial for his wealth and luxurious banquets.

houri   a seductively beautiful woman.

CHARACTER ANALYSES

Edna Pontellier

As the main protagonist, Edna undergoes a significant change in attitude, behavior, and overall character throughout the course of the novel, as she becomes aware of and examines the private, unvoiced thoughts that constitute her true self. Her characterization was strikingly ambivalent for its time: She is neither a flawless heroine nor a fallen woman, and her rebellion seems motivated more by the self-centered desire to fulfill her whims and wishes than to battle for a great cause larger than herself.

Edna is initially symbolized by the caged green-and-yellow parrot of the opening scene, the parrot that insists, in French, that everyone "go away, for God's sake." Like the parrot, Edna begins to desire solitude, pushing away her husband and former friends to achieve time alone in which she can work on her art or engage in self-reflection.

From the start, she is different from her husband and all her friends because she is a Presbyterian from Kentucky rather than a Creole Catholic. Physically, she is different from other women with her distinctive face and figure. Also, unlike the other women by whom she is surrounded, she is not a mother-woman, one who is willing to sacrifice her very self to her husband, children, and household.

Although not a particularly strong or rebellious spirit in the past, during her summer on Grand Isle, Edna develops a devotion to the pursuit of passion and sensuality, two qualities lacking in her marriage and home. She has a great weakness for the melodrama of unrequited or unfulfilled love. The passion she develops for Robert over the summer becomes her all-consuming occupation and, in part, instigates her radical departures from convention upon returning to New Orleans. Her obsession with Robert is ultimately suspect in its sincerity, given her instinctive attraction to adversity in love.

Also key in her development are Mademoiselle Reisz's piano performances, which stir up great emotions in Edna and both feed and enflame her need for some drama in her life. Edna's days at the racetrack function in the same way: Intoxicated by success at betting on the horses, she is reluctant to come back down to earth.

Out of that desire for stimulation comes a meaningless but sexually charged affair with Alcée Arobin. While she has no romantic feelings for him, she feels a potent physical attraction to him, an attraction that results in a sexual awakening just as Mademoiselle Reisz's piano performances brought about an emotional awakening.

Seeking to improve her skills as an artist is another result of her increasing need for self-fulfillment. As she begins to act in accordance with her own desires rather than with upper-class society's expectations, her illustrations and paintings "grow in force and individuality." She could not become a great artist, however, because she is not focused or ambitious enough to work when depressed or in gloomy weather, a limitation indicative of her poor grasp of resolutions and endings.

Throughout the novel, Edna never looks ahead to the consequences of her actions for herself or anyone else or how the situations she creates will resolve themselves. For example, when arranging to rent her own little house, she does not seem to be conscious of the fact that she is leaving her husband, thinking only that when Léonce returned there "would have to be an understanding, an explanation. Conditions would some way adjust themselves." Only at the end of the novel, at Madame Ratignolle's dramatic insistence, does she consider the effect of her actions on her sons.

Overall, Edna's spirit is strong enough to begin a rebellion but too weak to maintain it, although some readers have interpreted her suicide as a triumphant escape from those personal and social forces that she perceived as enslaving her.

Léonce Pontellier

Edna's materialistic husband remains in the dark throughout the novel: He does not perceive her obsession with Robert Lebrun or dissatisfaction with himself, and fails to grasp that she has left him when she rents her own house and moves out of his mansion. His intense focus on his business blinds him to the emotional process of growth and self-realization that his wife is undergoing. He considers his wife more of a possession or an employee than a person, and treats her accordingly.

When she performs the highly controversial act of abandoning her reception day because she does not feel like entertaining visitors, his reaction is based entirely on how her actions will affect his business prospects. His goals are strictly financial and superficial; he wants to "keep up with the procession" that is the upper-class life.

Léonce feels that he can buy favor with money, replacing kindness or sensitivity toward his wife with elaborate gifts. To Léonce's credit, he assiduously follows Dr. Mandelet's advice to give Edna free rein with her whims, even though her behavior disturbs him greatly. But he is still no match for the increasingly individualistic Edna. His ideal wife is a mother-woman such as Madame Ratignolle, a role that Edna can no longer bring herself to play.

Robert Lebrun

Robert has a romantic image of himself that is not supported by his actions or behavior. When he tells Edna about the Gulf ghost who returns to the coast every year waiting for a woman to wins his heart, he is implicitly talking about himself. Every summer Robert leaves his modest job in New Orleans to live with his mother at the *pension*, and courts a different woman each summer. His attentions are never serious, however; he targets married or older women who cannot truly respond to his mock courting. As insubstantial as a ghost, he lacks the emotional maturity to pursue or consummate an actual relationship with an eligible woman.

Two years younger than Edna, his youth and inexperience show themselves in his tendency to state grand intentions but not follow through on them, such as his legendary determination to go to Mexico to make his fortune. When he finds that he has become thoroughly infatuated with Edna, he is motivated by fear of true involvement to actually make the trip to Mexico but returns to New Orleans when the venture becomes too much work.

Yet he is charming and charismatic: "There was not one but was ready to follow when he led the way." His manner appeals to Edna's love of sensuality and desire for imaginative living, and he treats her with great chivalry.

Ultimately, however, he can only play-act the role of husband or lover. Robert does not have a brave, defiant soul, as does Edna. Although enthralled by her newly acquired power of seduction, he is overwhelmed by her declaration that "we shall love each other . . . Nothing else in the world is of any consequence," and is gone when she returns from Madame Ratignolle's, unable yet again to follow through, or to face the personal and social consequences should they consummate their love.

Mademoiselle Reisz

Although Mademoiselle Reisz is not introduced until Chapter IX, she is represented in the novel's opening scene by the mockingbird. Chopin describes the parrot (which symbolizes Edna) as speaking "a language which nobody understood, unless it was the mockingbird that hung on the other side of the door." Madame Reisz's piano playing speaks to Edna's soul as if that music were the language her soul had been waiting in silence for, awakening grand passions in Edna's soul and sparking her later rebellion.

Mockingbirds have a reputation as obnoxious birds, and Madame Reisz shares a similar reputation as a rude, ill-tempered woman. The description of the mockingbird also sets the tone for Madame Reisz's independent behavior within the confines of the insistently polite upper-class Creole society; she too whistles her own tune "with maddening persistence." Mademoiselle Reisz's isolation, both physical and social, provides more time for her art and herself. Although she leads a solitary life without friends or family in a dingy, dirty apartment, she has learned to live with the bad that accompanies the good, enduring the physical and societal limitations of a single woman who insists on telling the truth in exchange for living on her own terms.

Performing on piano is not mere entertainment or domestic decoration for Mademoiselle Reisz as it is for Madame Ratignolle. As a serious musician herself, Mademoiselle Reisz is doubtful that Edna is strong enough to become a true artist. Her definition of an artist as a "brave . . . soul that dares and defies" becomes a major theme of the novel. When she tests Edna metaphorically, physically feeling for her symbolic wings, and warns her about the fate of those souls who end up "bruised, exhausted, fluttering back to earth," she foreshadows Edna's final scene on the Grand Isle beach where a bird with a broken wing is sinking ominously through the air to its death in the water.

CRITICAL ESSAYS

Art in Edna Pontellier's Life

Like the rest of Edna's character, her identity as a painter is not clear cut. She is neither a recreational artist like Madame Ratignolle, whose musicianship is another element of consummate domesticity, nor a serious artiste like Mademoiselle Reisz, who has a piano rather than a personal life. The progress Edna makes in her paintings and illustrations is more of an indication of her growth than a catalyst for it. Instead, it is music that engenders change in Edna, inciting her to experience great passions otherwise lacking in her daily life. In that sense, art does play a pivotal role in her emotional and personal awakening but Edna hardly represents the archetypal artist.

The Effect of Music

An evaluation of the role of music in Edna's life requires a comparison of her two friends, both musicians who play for her: Madame Ratignolle and Mademoiselle Reisz. Each woman represents a path Edna can take in pursuit of her art and her independence.

Edna always enjoyed listening to Madame Ratignolle play the piano; the pieces invoked certain mental images that represented the music's theme. Yet because Madame Ratignolle's played sentimental pieces in a rather mundane fashion, the images Edna envisioned were rather mundane, as well—a woman stroking a cat or children at play. When she hears Mademoiselle Reisz play, the powerful artistry of the performance causes her to experience viscerally the extraordinary passions of the piece rather than forming a sentimental image of those emotions. Once back in New Orleans, she comes to prefer Mademoiselle Reisz's violently emotion-provoking performances in the dingy apartment to Madame Ratignolle's domesticated performances at her fashionable soiree musicales. Madame Ratignolle plays it safe with her music and her emotions; Edna is ready to gamble with her emotions and her life.

Note that Edna's death is foreshadowed by the Zampa duet played continuously throughout the summer by the Farival twins. The twins' performances represent the shackles of domesticity: All the Grand Isle vacationers must pretend to enjoy these endlessly repeated recitals due to the social convention that requires children and their actions to be evaluated entirely with sentiment rather than with honesty. At the gathering where the twins perform the Zampa duet yet again, the parrot (who represents Edna) squawks loudly its phrase "Go away, for God's sake!" as if voicing everyone's silent protest, a scene that represents Edna's later candor about doing what she truly feels like doing rather than what is expected of her. Note, too, that in this same scene, Mademoiselle Reisz is introduced, shown objecting to a crying baby. This scene implies that the necessary honesty of art is at odds with the sentimentality Edna's culture attaches to motherhood.

Ultimately, Mademoiselle Reisz becomes her mentor in the world of art, providing the definition of an artist and warning Edna about beginning but not finishing a rebellion. Edna is not enough of an artist to make it her reason for living when all else seems lost—unlike Mademoiselle Reisz, who sacrificed everything for her music and has received little in return. She has even molded her body to meet the demands of her art, even though that means when she plays "her body settled into ungraceful curves . . . that gave it an appearance of deformity." In contrast, Madame Ratignolle bends music to her purpose of "brightening the home and making it attractive."

Edna's Own Art

Just as Edna's character is neither all good nor all bad, as an artist, she is neither a brilliant painter nor a talentless hack. One key difference between Edna and a serious visual artist is that Edna does not use her art to express her discontent. On her bad days, "when life appeared to her like a grotesque pandemonium," she is not inspired by the darkness of human experience and emotion, as the great painters are. She can paint only when she is happily alive and reveling in the sensuality of existence.

While she does not seek to become a great artist, focusing instead on the satisfaction she feels in the process of creation itself, she is devoted to spending her time as her own person rather than as a possession or employee of Léonce. She persists in her art despite Léonce's criticism and Mademoiselle Reisz's friendly but authentic derision. Mademoiselle Reisz warns her about the fate of those who seek to "soar above the level plain of tradition and prejudice" but who lack the fortitude to maintain flight. Relating her words to Arobin later, Edna remarks "I'm not thinking of any extraordinary flights." This response indicates Edna's utter lack of ambition and foresight; distracted by thoughts of Robert, she does not heed the warning. Meanwhile, her focus on process over result almost allows her to have the best of both worlds: the freedom of Mademoiselle Reisz with the security of Madame Ratignolle. Part of the novel's message, however, is that she cannot have it all.

Edna admits her lack of artistry to Léonce, agreeing with his assessment that she is not, in fact, a true painter. "It isn't on account of painting that I let things go," she tells him. She is not driven to rebel so that she can pursue art; she just has more time for it after she decides to place her desire for solitude before all other external demands. Most importantly, her *atelier* (studio or workshop) at the top of the house provides her with a private place within her home. Léonce has his own office retreat but doesn't see the value of a private sanctuary for Edna. He wants her, instead, to spend more time in the main rooms of the house directing the domestic traffic.

Yet Edna breaks interesting ground in her little studio. There is rebellion in her choice of subject: Calling her children up to the atelier to sketch them was safe and predictable for a woman painter but making the quadroon the subject of a portrait—in Louisiana, in the 1890s—was a daring move, unprecedented for actual artists at the time. Then Edna brings up the maid, Ellen, for a portrait and has her loosen her hair from the protective housemaid's cap—a vote for impractical sensuality over domestic practicality.

Such bold steps taken confidently impact her work positively: Her teacher-turned-broker, Laidpore, is able to sell her paintings and illustrations as her work "grows in force and individuality." Her art enables her, in part, to support herself financially, to fund her independence. The sale of her paintings therefore helps to liberate her from Léonce: By refusing his bounty, she frees herself from his definition of her as one of his possessions.

Like her passion for Robert, art is an escapist venture for Edna because of her devotion to process over product. Ultimately, Edna does not pursue art as a means to achieve self-realization or provide insight about the world around her but merely to escape that world.

Wing Imagery in *The Awakening*

Chopin drew on a long history of bird imagery in women's writing to establish *The Awakening*'s opening image: the green-and-yellow parrot. Women writers since the 1700s had used caged birds as symbols to represent the limitations of their own domestic lives. Chopin's parrot, which symbolizes Edna, not only voices a desire for solitude (a condition necessary for creation of art and pursuit of self-knowledge) but at the same time represents the pressure exerted by both individuals and society in general for everyone to follow the same rules and display the same behavior. When her story begins, Edna obeys this implicit rule to go along with the crowd but later, as she begins to come into contact with her true self, she behaves as her moods and whims dictate rather than doing what everyone else does, such as when she abandons her reception day. Chopin herself detested parrots because they imitate what they hear instead of singing their own song.

Hanging in a cage on the other side of the door from the parrot is a mockingbird, who symbolizes the outspoken Mademoiselle Reisz, the only character to truly understand Edna's desire to achieve independence in thought and action. Although faced with her own limitations, as a single woman with little money, Mademoiselle Reisz wings defiantly away from the conventions that would impede her pursuit of art.

Chopin also uses wing imagery in her characterization of mother-women: "They were women . . . esteemed it a holy privilege to efface themselves as individuals and grow wings as ministering angels." This angel image contrasts sharply with the bad-tempered parrot and its caged compatriot, the mockingbird, as do the very personalities of those characters they represent. The mother-women willingly allow their angel wings to be clipped by their way of life, made unsuitable for flight, in exchange for the security that accompanies their roles. As wives of wealthy businessmen, they are rewarded for carrying out their domesticated role with a place in upper-class society, lovely homes, fine clothes, and all of the other privileges and prestige that accompany their social position. Yet their acceptance of these rewards makes them beholden to their husbands, ensuring their dependence.

Note that when Léonce becomes tired of listening to the parrot's loudly repeated phrases and the mockingbird's persistent whistling, he has "the privilege of quitting [the birds'] society when they ceased to be entertaining." Meanwhile, the birds can only protest as best they can when the environment in which their cages hang becomes unacceptable to them, such as when the parrot seems to be objecting to listening yet again to the Farival twins play their oft-repeated duets on piano. Like Edna, the parrot is censured for his honesty by those who have a sentimental need to maintain certain appearances of civility or enthusiasm, despite their true feelings about the situation. Tired of effacing her own innate self to carry out the mother-woman role, Edna breaks with all social expectation when she exercises her "privilege of quitting" Léonce's company by moving into the so-called pigeon house. Note that while she has made progress in that she has escaped Léonce's gilded cage, still she is defined as a domesticated bird.

A critical use of the bird imagery is Mademoiselle Reisz's symbolic assessment of Edna's wings, an incident Edna describes to Arobin: Mademoiselle Reisz "felt my shoulder blades, to see if my wings were strong," and warned that those individuals who would "soar above the level plain of tradition and prejudice must have strong wings" lest they find themselves unable to complete their flight and fall to their death. Such an image evokes the legend of Icarus, who achieved flight with a set of manufactured wings but fell to his death in the sea when out of pride he flew too high, and the sun melted the wax that held the feathers to his artificial wings. Interestingly, when *The Awakening* was first published, some reviewers not only condemned the book, but also insisted that Edna's death was well deserved because she was selfish enough to value her journey to self-realization over her household and family.

CliffsNotes Review

Use this CliffsNotes Review to test your understanding of the original text and reinforce what you've learned in this book. After you work through the review and essay questions and the fun and useful practice projects, you're well on your way to understanding a comprehensive and meaningful interpretation of *The Awakening*.

Q&A

1. Who is Robert's business partner in Mexico?

2. In what army and war did Edna's father, the Colonel, serve?

3. How does the parrot symbolize Edna?

   a. Edna tends to repeat stock phrases rather than speak her mind.

   b. Edna's free spirit is caged by her family and society.

   c. Léonce will leave Edna if she annoys him too much, just as he avoids the parrot.

4. Why is Mademoiselle Reisz disliked by almost everyone?

   a. She lacks fashion sense.

   b. She lives in a shabby apartment.

   c. She gives her true opinions instead of being polite.

Answers: (1) Montel, an old family friend. (2) The Confederate Army in the Civil War. (3) b. (4) c.

Identify the Quote

1. *"Allez vous-en! Sapristi!"* meaning "Go away, for God's sake!"

2. "[S]ometimes I feel this summer as if I were walking through the green meadow again; idly, aimlessly, unthinking, and unguided."

3. "[W]e've got to observe *les convenances* if we ever expect to get on and keep up with the procession."

4. "Oh think of the children! Remember them!"

5. "[O]ne is really forced as a matter of convenience these day to assume the virtue of an occupation if he has it not."

6. [H]e loves you, poor fool, and is trying to forget you.

Answers: (1) The parrot's oft-repeated French phrase. (2) Edna Pontellier, to Madame Ratignolle. (3) Léonce Pontellier, to Edna. (4) Madame Ratignolle, to Edna. (5) Alcée Arobin, at the dinner party. (6) Mademoiselle Reisz, to Edna, about Robert.

Essay Questions

1. To what extent does Edna's story depend upon its location in 1890s America? How might her behavior and attitudes be received in another place and time, such as in ancient Greece or medieval England?

2. What is Edna trying to achieve throughout the novel? Does she fulfill her mission?

3. Identify and discuss the bird/wings imagery used throughout the book.

4. How do music and art function within the novel and in Edna's life?

5. What role do children play in this novel? How is Edna like a child, and how do her own children affect her decision to kill herself?

Practice Projects

1. Create a Web site to introduce *The Awakening* to other readers. Design pages to intrigue and inform your audience and invite other readers to post their thoughts and responses to their reading of the novel.

2. Develop a screenplay for a film version of the book. Indicate which scenes you'd depict, which actors you'd like to cast, and so on.

3. Put together a discussion panel with a diverse group of people; each person should answer the question "What would you do if you were Edna?". Present the group's responses to the class.

CliffsNotes Resource Center

The learning doesn't need to stop here. CliffsNotes Resource Center shows you the best of the best—links to the best information in print and online about the author and/or related works. And don't think that this is all we've prepared for you; we've put all kinds of pertinent information at www.cliffsnotes.com. Look for all the terrific resources at your favorite bookstore or local library and on the Internet. When you're online, make your first stop www.cliffsnotes.com where you'll find more incredibly useful information about *The Awakening*.

Books

This CliffsNotes book provides a meaningful interpretation of *The Awakening* published by Wiley Publishing, Inc. If you are looking for information about the author and/or related works, check out these other publications:

HAROLD BLOOM, ed. *Kate Chopin.* New York: Chelsea House Publishers, 1987. Bloom's introduction addresses the influence of Walt Whitman on *The Awakening.* The ten other essays address the full body of Chopin's work.

LYNDA S. BOREN and SARA deSAUSSURE DAVIS, editors. *Kate Chopin Reconsidered: Beyond the Bayou.* Baton Rouge: Louisiana State University Press, 1992. These essays about Chopin's life and work focus mostly on *The Awakening* and Chopin's development of its principal themes in other stories.

JOYCE DYER. *The Awakening: A Novel of Beginnings.* New York: Twayne Publishers, 1993. Dyer presents a chronology of Chopin's life and work, plus nine essays, three of which focus on the novel's literary and historical context.

ALICE HALL PETRY. *Critical Essays on Kate Chopin.* New York: G.K. Hall and Co., 1996. This book presents reviews of Chopin's work by her contemporaries and by scholars throughout the twentieth century.

EMILY TOTH. *Unveiling Kate Chopin.* Jackson: University Press of Mississippi, 1999. This vivid biography makes connections between the people and events in Chopin's life with her characters and stories. Included are photos.

It's easy to find books published by Wiley Publishing, Inc. You'll find them in your favorite bookstores (on the Internet and at a store near you). We also have three Web sites that you can use to read about all the books we publish:

- www.cliffsnotes.com

- www.dummies.com

- www.wiley.com

Internet

Check out these Web resources for more information about Kate Chopin and *The Awakening*:

Exploring Kate Chopin's The Awakening, www.vcu.edu/engweb/eng384/awake.htm—This site spells out major motifs and symbols, and relays interpretations of Edna's suicide. Included in the links are photos of Grand Isle.

A Guide to Internet Resources for Kate Chopin's The Awakening, http://soleil.acomp.usf.edu/~smasturz/—This site's unique feature is its guidelines on developing and researching a literary thesis, plus excellent material on Chopin and her work.

Domestic Goddesses, www.womenwriters.net/domesticgoddess/—An e-journal devoted to nineteenth century women writers who wrote fiction revolving around women's issues and topics, this site includes a great section on Chopin.

Kate Chopin: A Re-Awakening, www.pbs.org/katechopin/—This PBS site contains the full transcript of the June 1999 documentary on Kate Chopin.

Next time you're on the Internet, don't forget to drop by www.cliffsnotes.com. We created an online Resource Center that you can use today, tomorrow, and beyond.

Index